For giada, a good m

pleasure in cooking for those you love, and slowing down to embrace every moment spent at the table. In *Giada's Italy,* she returns to her native Rome to reconnect with the flavors that have inspired the way she cooks and shares what it means to live *la dolce vita.* Here she shares recipes for authentic Italian dishes as her family has prepared them for years, updated with her signature flavors. Her Bruschetta with Burrata and Kale Salsa Verde is a perfect light dinner or lunch, and Grilled Swordfish with Candied Lemon Salad can be prepared in minutes for a quick weeknight meal. Sartu di Riso is a showstopping entrée best made with help from the family, and because no meal is complete without something sweet, Giada's Italian-inflected desserts like Pound Cake with Limoncello Zabaglione and Chianti Affogato will keep everyone lingering at the table just a little bit longer. Filled with stunning photography taken in and around Rome, intimate family shots and stories, and more recipes than ever before, *Giada's Italy* will make you fall in love with Italian cooking all over again.

giada's italy

giada's
ITALY

GIADA DE LAURENTIIS

my
recipes
for
LA
DOLCE
VITA

CLARKSON POTTER/PUBLISHERS
NEW YORK

crownpublishing.com
clarksonpotter.com

CLARKSON POTTER is a trademark and
POTTER with colophon is a registered
trademark of Penguin Random House LLC.

Library of Congress Cataloging-in-
Publication Data is available

ISBN 978-0-307-98722-8
eBook ISBN 978-0-307-98723-5

Printed in China

Book and cover design by Marysarah Quinn
Photographs by Aubrie Pick

10 9 8 7 6 5 4 3 2 1

First Edition

FOR MY FAMILY
who instilled Italian traditions
in me, even when we lived
in the United States,
and for everyone who loves
Italian culture and wants to feel
like an honorary Italian

contents

introduction   9

the italian pantry   12

STARTERS   *19*

LUNCH   *50*

IN-BETWEENS   *79*

WEEKNIGHTS   *107*

LA DOLCE VITA   *157*

SIDES   *213*

SWEETS   *247*

acknowledgments   *283*

index   *285*

introduction

For years I've defined the kind of cooking I do as Italian . . . with a California twist. So many of the dishes I love best reflect an appreciation of classic Italian home cooking instilled in me from a young age by my grandfather Dino. Today, I am still inspired by many of these dishes, and it's fun to reinterpret them for my daughter, Jade, as well as for my restaurant and television shows. My versions may be a bit lighter or a little healthier, in keeping with the way most of us want to eat today, but at their cores, these dishes are authentically Italian in spirit.

For the past two years I've had the incredible good fortune to be able to shoot my show *Giada in Italy* on location, first in the beautiful coastal community of Positano and then in Florence, a cosmopolitan city in the heart of Tuscany. Spending extended periods in my home country for the first time since I was a little girl was like recharging some essential batteries I hadn't even realized were run down. And while the food was comfortingly familiar, the culture was strikingly different from my day-to-day life at home in the States. Seeing the pleasure that Italian home cooks take in every aspect of preparing meals—from visiting the market to search out the very best ingredients, to infusing every dish they cook with their own personality and "secret" touches, to embracing every moment spent at the table as an opportunity for love, laughter, and emotional connection—helped me to get in touch all over again with what I love about cooking. Italians know how to take their time, slow down, and appreciate what they've made—and the people they are sharing it with. It's a lesson we can't learn too often.

With my suitcases long since unpacked and the pounding surf of the Pacific Ocean rather than the warm waters of the Mediterranean Sea beckoning me on weekends, I still try to embrace those lessons in cooking from the heart every day, and bring a little taste of *la dolce vita* to everything I make. At the same time, I'm mindful of the realities most of us face when it comes to preparing meals, especially during the week, when life can get so hectic that cooking falls to the bottom of a long list of priorities. As a working mother with a demanding day job, I'm all too familiar with the challenges involved in creating wholesome, inviting meals on a daily basis. So, in the recipes that follow, I make allowances for a few good-quality convenience foods when I don't think they will compromise the final outcome of a dish, and I stay away from ingredients, no matter how authentically Italian, if I think you'll have to hunt high and low to find them. Who needs that extra stress? Most important, I occasionally tiptoe outside the confines of strictly authentic Italian cooking to take advantage of the extraordinary variety of foods and flavors available to American cooks, using them in ways that I know even the most traditional Italian cooks—even Nonno Dino—would approve of.

With this book I've broken the recipes into chapters that reflect the way Italians (myself included) like to eat. That said, these categories are just suggestions. Some of my favorite light suppers are in the Lunch and Starters chapters, and many of the "in-betweens" are great for the cocktail hour. I've added suggestions throughout for pairing dishes to make complete menus, but you should mix and match as you like best.

LUNCH: These lighter, simpler meals include soups, salads, and more casual dishes that are still satisfying.

IN-BETWEENS: This chapter explains a lot about Italians and how they view mealtimes—and the time in between. For Italians, pizza, a crostini, or a panini is something to eat as a midafternoon pick-me-up, not the main event. Growing up, we used to have pizza as an appetizer when dinner was served on the late side, and a crostini or even a panini was my usual after-school snack.

WEEKNIGHTS: These dishes are fast, easy, and comforting.

LA DOLCE VITA: These more traditional dishes may take a bit longer to prepare (although much of the cooking time will be unattended).

Like me, the recipes in this book are Italian through and through, yet completely at home in an American kitchen. I hope they will help you channel the spirit of those big-hearted Italian cooks and rediscover the simple pleasures of feeding food you feel good about to the people you care about.

the italian pantry

Italians consider grocery shopping an integral part of the cooking process and buy perishables like fish, meat, cheese, and produce nearly every day, relying on a limited but essential store of pantry goods to round out their meals. While few of us have the luxury of time to shop that often, it still makes sense to keep some flavor enhancers on hand to avoid last-minute dashes to the gourmet food store when you're ready to cook.

We've come a long way since the days when you had to hunt for sun-dried tomatoes and the only grated Italian cheese stocked in most grocery stores came in a green shaker-top canister. Ingredients that were once considered exotic are now readily available, and in most well-stocked markets, you'll have your pick of good-quality extra-virgin olive oils, imported pastas, rustic country breads, and other Italian staples. For that reason, and because I know how annoying it is to get ready to make a recipe only to discover you're missing a key ingredient, I've kept specialty foods to a minimum in the recipes that follow, and when possible, I've suggested substitutions for ingredients that might not be as easy to get your hands on.

Nonetheless, there is a small handful of products I would hate to cook without, and I find the extra effort needed to track them down online or at a specialty food store saves me time in the long run, because they offer so much big, authentic flavor that you really can't duplicate any other way. Here is my short-and-sweet pantry list.

CALABRIAN CHILE PASTE: If you pick only one thing to buy from this list, make it this one. I throw this blend of crushed dried chiles and extra-virgin olive oil into everything, from pasta sauces and stews to salad dressings for a bit of mellow heat. It's usually found online or in a specialty store, but it's well worth seeking out; one jar will last you a long time. Crushed red pepper flakes can be substituted.

PARMESAN CHEESE RINDS: This invaluable flavoring element adds depth to soups, stews, and stocks. Save your rinds or look for containers of rinds if your market has a good-size cheese department and sells a lot of grated cheese.

FINOCCHIONA: A type of salami common in Tuscany that is flavored with fennel. It can be replaced with regular salami. Store in the refrigerator as you would any sliced meat.

TUNA AND ANCHOVIES: Choose the oil-packed Italian type in jars for the best flavor.

CASTELVETRANO OLIVES: A bright green olive from Sicily with a buttery flavor that is more sweet than briny. Substitute any mild-flavored olive.

CHEESES: Aside from a really good Parmigiano-Reggiano for grating, you won't have to look far for the cheeses used in this book, but there are a couple that might be new to you: *ciliegine* and *burrata*. These mild

cheeses—both related to mozzarella—are a visual upgrade from the standard 8-ounce ball you'd slice for a caprese salad. Ciliegine takes its name from little cherries, and these balls are about one-quarter the size of bocconcini, which can be substituted for them. Soft, delicate burrata has an oozy, creamy interior that makes it extra delicious smeared on a crostini or tossed with hot pasta. Smoked scamorza is a bit firmer and drier than smoked mozzarella, which can be used in its place and has a similar dusky smoked flavor.

SPECK: Like prosciutto, speck is a cured ham, the main difference being that speck is lightly smoked and prosciutto is not. They can be used interchangeably.

There are other pantry items you will encounter throughout this book that are more easily found and are always smart to have on hand: a good olive oil for cooking, plus an extra-virgin oil for drizzling and using in recipes that are not subjected to heat, like dressings, salads, and crostini; balsamic vinegar (both red and white); long and short pastas (cock's comb–shaped *creste di gallo* is a current favorite); pearled farro; jarred roasted peppers, preferably the smaller, sweeter piquillo peppers; smoked paprika (both dolce and picante); quick-cooking polenta; pink peppercorns; flake salt such as Maldon; and, of course, mascarpone cheese.

"Appetizers" sounds so formal and really undersells the versatility of the dishes in this chapter, many of which are simple, light bites that work in lots of different ways. Unless I'm testing a recipe, it's rare that I'll make a separate first course just for me and Jade. That said, I like to keep dips and crostini toppings in the fridge for impromptu snacks or company, and they are also a great option when you need to bring something for a potluck. I don't really eat much for lunch, but I usually get hungry around three in the afternoon, and a dip like the avocado white bean spread on page 25 is the perfect solution. When I have friends over, though, I usually do take the time to start the meal with something small but tasty, whether a plated dish or smaller nibbles to tide them over while the main event finishes cooking. Though light, these dishes offer plenty of concentrated flavor, and many nights I would be very happy with a bowl of the Pan-Roasted Clams on page 42 and a green salad. So don't come to this chapter only when you're hosting a big party; you'll find lots of occasions when one of these recipes is just right.

starters

POTATO CRISPS WITH GOAT CHEESE AND OLIVES

GRILLED ARTICHOKES WITH ANCHOVY MAYONNAISE

AVOCADO WHITE BEAN DIP

BURRATA WITH NECTARINES AND CORN

ANTIPASTI IN A JAR

CANDIED PROSCIUTTO

PARMIGIANO-REGGIANO AND PROSCIUTTO SPICED PRUNES

GRAPPA-POACHED PEARS WITH SPECK

APRICOT MOSTARDA

SPICY CALABRIAN SHRIMP

PAN-ROASTED CLAMS

CRAB ARANCINI

HAM AND RICOTTA PINWHEELS

potato crisps with goat cheese and olives

YIELD:
MAKES ABOUT 60 CRISPS

SERVE WITH:
GRAPPA-POACHED PEARS WITH SPECK

These are a fun twist on a crostini, and everyone is always impressed when I make potato chips from scratch, even though it's actually super easy. The trick is to use a mandoline to get uniform and ultrathin slices. If you're not up for frying, just spread the cheese and tapenade on small rounds of toasted bread.

FOR THE CRISPS

1 to 2 cups vegetable oil

3 medium Yukon Gold potatoes

Freshly ground black pepper

FOR THE CHEESE

¼ cup fresh goat cheese, at room temperature

¼ cup mascarpone cheese, at room temperature

½ teaspoon grated orange zest (from ½ orange)

FOR THE OLIVE SPREAD

½ cup pitted Castelvetrano olives

½ cup pitted kalamata olives

1 tablespoon capers, drained and rinsed

1 teaspoon chopped fresh rosemary

2 tablespoons extra-virgin olive oil

MAKE THE CRISPS: Heat ½ inch of vegetable oil in a medium saucepan over medium heat. Slice the potatoes ⅛ inch thick using a mandoline. When the oil reaches 350°F on a deep-fry thermometer, add a small handful of sliced potatoes to the oil (you'll need to cook them in batches, as overcrowding the pan will cause the chips to curl). Fry each batch about 4 minutes, or until the potatoes are crispy and golden brown. Using a wire skimmer or slotted spoon, remove the potatoes to a paper towel–lined tray and drain well. Season with a few grinds of black pepper. Continue with the remaining potatoes.

MAKE THE CHEESE: Use a rubber spatula to mix together the goat cheese, mascarpone, and orange zest until smooth and well combined. Set aside at room temperature.

MAKE THE OLIVE SPREAD: Place the Castelvetranos, kalamatas, capers, and rosemary in the bowl of a food processor. Pulse to chop finely. Add the olive oil and blend until the mixture is very finely chopped; it should still have a little texture but be cohesive.

TO ASSEMBLE, place a dollop of the cheese spread on a chip and top with a spoonful of the olive spread.

grilled artichokes with anchovy mayonnaise

When it's artichoke season, there's no better way to serve them than grilled on a stovetop grill pan, as here, or outdoors. Whether plated as a first course or offered at a casual buffet, they look fancy but, honestly, are just so easy to prepare. Mustard and anchovy paste make this mayo slightly spicy and tangy and perfectly salty.

YIELD:
SERVES 4

SERVE WITH:
FLANK STEAK WITH ROASTED GRAPES AND MUSHROOMS

PREPARE THE ARTICHOKES: Trim the artichokes by slicing off the stems and the top quarter of each artichoke. Break off and discard the tough outer leaves, peel the bases, and use scissors to snip off any sharp leaf tips. Halve the trimmed artichokes vertically and use a small spoon to scoop out the furry choke from the center of each.

In a medium Dutch oven, combine the white wine, rosemary, bay leaf, and ½ teaspoon of the salt with 1 cup of water. Squeeze the juice from each lemon half into the pot and add the lemon halves as well. Place the artichokes in the pot, cut-side down. Cover the pot and bring the liquid to a simmer over medium-high heat, then reduce the heat to maintain a gentle simmer. Cook for 10 to 15 minutes, or until the tip of a paring knife easily pierces the thickest part of the artichoke. Drain the artichokes on a wire rack.

PREPARE THE MAYONNAISE: In the bowl of a food processor, combine the mayonnaise, garlic, anchovy paste, mustard, and olive oil. Puree until smooth. Add the mint and pulse to combine. Let the flavors marry for 15 minutes or so.

Preheat a grill pan over medium-high heat.

Drizzle the artichokes with the olive oil and sprinkle with the remaining ¼ teaspoon salt. Grill the artichokes, cut-side down, for about 4 minutes, or until nicely browned on the cut side. Turn and grill for another 2 minutes, pressing down gently to ensure a little browning. Serve with the anchovy mayonnaise for dipping.

FOR THE ARTICHOKES

2 artichokes

1 cup dry white wine

3 fresh rosemary sprigs

1 bay leaf

¾ teaspoon kosher salt

1 lemon, halved

1 tablespoon olive oil

FOR THE ANCHOVY MAYONNAISE

½ cup mayonnaise

1 garlic clove, smashed and peeled

½ teaspoon anchovy paste

1 teaspoon Dijon mustard

1 tablespoon olive oil

1 tablespoon chopped fresh mint

avocado white bean dip

You find cannellini bean dips in restaurants everywhere in Italy, where they are offered with bread before the meal. Adding avocado makes the dip even creamier and more luxurious. I always seem to have these ingredients in my pantry and refrigerator, so I make it often when friends stop by. It's also a great dish to bring to someone's house because it travels well.

YIELD:
SERVES 6 TO 8

SERVE WITH:
ZUCCHINI SOTTOLIO ON CROSTINI
SPICY CALABRIAN SHRIMP

In the bowl of a food processor, combine the cannellini beans, avocados, salt, and lemon juice. Puree until the mixture is smooth, stopping once or twice to scrape down the sides with a rubber spatula. Add the basil and pulse to incorporate. Serve the dip surrounded by your preferred dippers.

1 (15-ounce) can cannellini beans, drained and rinsed

2 avocados, diced

1 teaspoon kosher salt

2 tablespoons lemon juice

⅓ cup chopped fresh basil

Cut vegetables, pita chips, or bread, for dipping

burrata with nectarines and corn

YIELD:
SERVES 4 TO 6

SERVE WITH:
**CRISPY CHICKEN THIGHS
PAN-SEARED BRANZINO WITH
TOMATO AND CAPERS**

During that short period when both nectarines and corn are in season at the same time, I make this almost every day. Sometimes the corn is so sweet I don't even cook it; otherwise I grill it briefly to bring the sugars to the surface. It's a casual, family-style starter, but honestly, I like it so much I'd make it my lunch and dinner! It's everything I love about summer food.

2 small ripe nectarines, cut into small wedges

⅓ cup chopped fresh basil

1 fresh Fresno or serrano chile, thinly sliced

2 teaspoons white balsamic vinegar

1 tablespoon extra-virgin olive oil, plus more as needed

½ teaspoon kosher salt

8 slices from a rustic Italian loaf

4 ears of corn, shucked and silk removed

8 ounces fresh burrata, drained and patted dry

½ teaspoon flake salt, such as Maldon

In a medium bowl, combine the nectarines, basil, chile, vinegar, 1 tablespoon olive oil, and the kosher salt, and combine gently. Set aside and let the mixture marinate for at least 30 minutes at room temperature or up to 2 hours in the refrigerator.

Heat a stovetop grill pan over medium-high heat. Brush the bread slices with oil and grill until lightly marked on both sides, 4 to 5 minutes total. Add the corn to the pan and grill on all sides until warmed with a few charred spots. Use a sharp knife to slice the kernels off the cobs and add them to the bowl with the nectarines.

To serve, spoon the nectarine mixture onto a platter. Tear the burrata into 8 to 12 good-size pieces and arrange them over the salad. Sprinkle the flake salt evenly over the cheese and drizzle the cheese with a little extra olive oil. Serve with the grilled bread.

antipasti in a jar

Although the ingredients are familiar, these jars make the standard antipasto fare—cheese, veggies, olives—a little more stylish and formal. I prepare them ahead of time and put one at each place setting when guests arrive, or you can set them out with toothpicks for people to share. I also like to bring a jar or two to a friend's dinner party as a hostess gift. The part I love most about these is that Jade enjoys both making them and eating them for lunch! And the longer this sits, the better it gets, so keep a couple assembled in the fridge.

YIELD:
MAKES 2 (10-OUNCE) JARS;
SERVES 2 TO 4

SERVE WITH:
ITALIAN SHEET-PAN CHICKEN
WITH BREAD SALAD
PENNE WITH PORK RAGU

In a small bowl, toss together the mozzarella, olive oil, ⅛ teaspoon salt, the oregano, and red pepper flakes. In a separate bowl, toss the tomatoes with the remaining ¼ teaspoon salt and the basil. Allow both mixtures to sit for 5 minutes so the flavors can marry.

Divide the marinated mozzarella balls evenly between two 10-ounce glass jars. Spoon the tomatoes over the cheese and top with the olives. Cover the jars with their lids and refrigerate until ready to serve, up to 3 days.

1 cup ciliegine (baby mozzarella balls)

1 tablespoon extra-virgin olive oil

⅛ teaspoon plus ¼ teaspoon kosher salt

¼ teaspoon dried oregano

¼ teaspoon crushed red pepper flakes

1 cup grape tomatoes, halved

2 tablespoons chopped fresh basil

½ cup pitted green olives

candied prosciutto

YIELD:
MAKES 5 OR 6 PIECES

SERVE WITH:
MARINATED OLIVES

If you like sweet/salty treats, you are going to find this addictive. The prosciutto gets crunchy and crispy, and because it's so thin, you can crumble it on a salad. I also make this for Jade as a snack and add it to my antipasto platters for a fun twist.

¼ pound thinly sliced prosciutto di San Daniele (5 or 6 thin slices)

2 tablespoons sugar

Pinch of cayenne pepper

⅛ teaspoon ground allspice

¼ teaspoon kosher salt

2 teaspoons extra-virgin olive oil

Preheat the oven to 350°F.

Line a rimmed baking sheet with parchment paper. Lay the slices of prosciutto on the parchment without overlapping them. In a small bowl, mix together the sugar, cayenne, allspice, and salt. Brush each slice of prosciutto with some olive oil and sprinkle with the spice mix.

Bake the prosciutto for 16 to 18 minutes, or until it is beginning to crisp and the sugar is caramelized. Transfer the slices to a wire rack to cool completely. Blot with a paper towel if beads of oil form on the prosciutto.

parmigiano-reggiano and prosciutto spiced prunes

YIELD:
MAKES 20 PRUNES

SERVE WITH:
**BAROLO-BRAISED SHORT RIBS
SARTU DI RISO**

This is an elegant appetizer from Tuscany. Decadent, salty, and nutty little bites, and the prunes get plump and juicy from the poaching liquid—plus it makes the house smell good!

½ cup port wine

2 tablespoons apple cider vinegar

3 whole cloves

1 cinnamon stick

3 strips of orange zest

¼ cup sugar

Pinch of kosher salt

20 pitted prunes

¼ pound Parmigiano-Reggiano, cut into bite-size pieces

5 thin slices prosciutto di Parma, each cut in 4 pieces

In a small saucepan, combine 1 cup of water with the port, vinegar, cloves, cinnamon, orange zest, sugar, and salt. Bring to a simmer over medium heat. Reduce the heat to medium-low and add the prunes. Simmer for about 10 minutes, or until the prunes have softened and plumped. Allow to cool in the liquid for 5 minutes. Using a slotted spoon, remove the prunes from the poaching liquid to a plate and allow them to cool completely.

Preheat the oven to 400°F.

Using a paring knife, make a slit from stem to tip in each of the prunes. Stuff the prunes with a piece of the Parmigiano-Reggiano. Wrap each prune in a quarter piece of prosciutto and place it, seam-side down, on a rimmed baking sheet. Bake for 8 to 10 minutes, or until the prosciutto is crispy and the Parmigiano-Reggiano is soft and melted. Serve warm or at room temperature.

aperitivi

If you travel to Italy, you may see that many bars and hotels offer aperitivi starting around 4 or 5 o'clock in the afternoon. This European tradition is something like American happy hour but without the half-price well drinks and chicken wings. Since Europeans tend to eat later, having a small bite and a drink in the downtime between work and the evening meal is a relaxing transition that puts you in the mood for a nice long dinner. If it's at someone's home, it's the time to get acquainted while working up an appetite for the meal to come. While most places offer a full bar, there is usually a specialty cocktail, something light like a spritz or wine drink like sangria. And you will always be offered a selection of savory snacks along with your drink. Potato chips—sturdy kettle chips, always plain, not flavored—smoked or salted almonds, and maybe a little bowl of marinated olives are standard aperitivi fare even at neighborhood bars, but some spots pride themselves on more elaborate offerings: sliced meats and salamis, mostarda with crackers, little bocconcini and baby tomatoes, tiny squares of quiche or bits of pressed sandwiches. Another slice of the sweet life worth bringing home with you!

grappa-poached pears with speck

If you enjoy serving melon and prosciutto in the summer months, try this cold-weather version with fall fruits and spices. Use petite Forelle pears, if you can find them, because they are the perfect size, but Bosc or Red Bartlett works well, too. Buy the pears a touch underripe because you don't want them to get too soft and fall apart when you cook them. You can substitute any kind of cured ham for the speck as long as it is very thinly sliced.

YIELD:
MAKES 24 BITES

SERVE WITH:
**LAMB OSSO BUCO
MUSHROOM AND ASPARAGUS
FARROTTO**

In a medium Dutch oven, combine 2 cups of water with the grappa, sugar, cloves, red pepper flakes, peppercorns, rosemary, orange zest, and salt. Bring to a simmer over medium heat, stirring occasionally with a wooden spoon to help dissolve the sugar. Simmer for 5 minutes. Carefully place the pears in the poaching liquid, cut-side down. Place a circle of parchment paper on top of the liquid to keep the pears submerged and continue to simmer gently for 15 to 20 minutes. Turn off the heat and allow the pears to cool completely in the liquid.

Cut each pear half into 4 wedges. Cut each piece of speck in half lengthwise. Bundle a few arugula leaves together with a pear wedge. Lay the bundle on one end of a halved piece of speck and roll the speck around the bundle; secure it with a toothpick. Repeat with the remaining pears, arugula, and speck.

2 cups grappa

½ cup sugar

8 whole cloves

⅛ teaspoon crushed red pepper flakes

8 black peppercorns

2 fresh rosemary sprigs

1 teaspoon grated orange zest

½ teaspoon kosher salt

3 small Forelle, Bosc, or Red Bartlett pears, peeled, halved, and cored

12 thin slices speck

1½ cups baby arugula

apricot mostarda

YIELD:
MAKES ABOUT 2 CUPS

SERVE WITH:
**CHEESE, SALAMI, MARCONA
ALMONDS
CANDIED PROSCIUTTO**

An antipasto platter is a quick, easy, and attractive way to feed a group, because most of the elements—cured meats, cheese, olives, breadsticks—are store-bought. To add a special touch, though, most Italians personalize the spread by including something homemade, like spiced nuts, marinated olives, or a sweet-savory fruit condiment known as mostarda. In Italy it's common to make condiments like this in large batches and preserve them for a longer shelf life, but even in the fridge, the tangy, spicy blend of dried fruit and mustard lasts for a month or so. It's fantastic with roast pork or even on yogurt. Spread the mostarda on crostini or a ham and Brie sandwich; its sharp flavor cuts through the fattiness.

1 tablespoon olive oil

1 shallot, finely chopped

¼ teaspoon kosher salt

1 teaspoon mustard seeds

½ teaspoon crushed red pepper flakes

½ cup white wine vinegar

5 tablespoons sugar

1 teaspoon Dijon mustard

2 cups dried Turkish apricots, chopped

Heat the olive oil in a small saucepan over medium heat. Add the shallot and salt. Cook for 1 minute, or until the shallots are fragrant and soft. Stir in the mustard seeds and red pepper flakes, and cook an additional minute. Add the vinegar and sugar. Bring to a simmer, stirring often, until the sugar is dissolved, about 3 minutes.

Whisk in the mustard and add 1 cup of the chopped apricots. Bring to a simmer and cook, stirring often, for about 10 minutes, or until the apricots are plump and the mixture has started to thicken to a jam-like consistency. Turn off the heat and stir in the remaining apricots. Cover the pan and cool to room temperature. Transfer the mostarda to one or more tightly covered containers and store in the refrigerator for up to 4 weeks. Serve at room temperature.

spicy calabrian shrimp

My version of a shrimp cocktail has a lot more kick than the steakhouse standard, thanks to Calabrian chile paste. I use this spicy condiment in many of my recipes; it's kind of like the Italian version of sriracha. If you can get your hands on fresh Thai basil, which has a slight licorice flavor, it is really nice here, but if not, regular basil is just fine.

YIELD:
SERVES 4 TO 6

SERVE WITH:
**VEAL SALTIMBOCA
MILANESE-STYLE
ASPARAGUS WITH GRILLED
MELON SALAD**

Preheat the oven to 425°F.

In a medium bowl, whisk together the Parmigiano-Reggiano, olive oil, chile paste, lemon zest, oregano, and salt. Add the shrimp and toss to coat. Allow the shrimp to marinate for 10 minutes at room temperature.

Spread the shrimp evenly on a rimmed baking sheet and bake for 8 to 10 minutes, or until the shrimp are pink and opaque all the way through. Sprinkle the lemon juice and basil over the shrimp. Serve warm.

½ cup freshly grated
Parmigiano-Reggiano

2 tablespoons olive oil

2 teaspoons Calabrian
chile paste

1 teaspoon grated lemon zest
(from ½ lemon)

¼ teaspoon dried oregano

¼ teaspoon kosher salt

1 pound large shrimp, peeled
and deveined, tails intact

1 tablespoon fresh lemon
juice

1 tablespoon chopped fresh
basil or Thai basil

pan-roasted clams

YIELD:
SERVES 4

SERVE WITH:
**PANE POMODORO
ENDIVE, PANCETTA, AND
TOMATO SALAD**

This dish truly transports me to the Amalfi coast. Citrus, clam broth, fresh herbs, and butter make an amazing dipping sauce for crusty bread. Yum! If you can't find cockles or tiny New Zealand clams choose the smallest littleneck clams you can get and cook a minute or two longer. This would also make a nice dinner for two.

2 pounds cockles or Manila clams, scrubbed and rinsed

2 tablespoons fresh flat-leaf parsley leaves

¼ cup (½ stick) unsalted butter

4 fresh thyme sprigs

1 teaspoon grated lemon zest

½ teaspoon grated orange zest

¼ teaspoon crushed red pepper flakes

Crusty bread, for dipping

Heat a large straight-sided skillet over high heat until hot. Add the clams and cover the skillet. Cook, shaking the pan every so often, for about 3 minutes, or until the clams are opened. Discard any unopened clams.

Remove the pan from the heat. Using a slotted spoon, scoop the clams into a serving bowl, leaving any juices in the skillet, and sprinkle the clams with the parsley leaves.

Add the butter, thyme, lemon zest, orange zest, and red pepper flakes to the pan with the clam juices, and place over medium heat. Warm until the butter is melted. Pour the sauce over the clams or serve it on the side with crusty bread.

crab arancini

In Italy, where risotto is served as both an entrée and a side dish, cooks often have some left over in the fridge and these little fritters are a good way to use it up. I like them so much I make risotto from scratch in the morning, let it cool all day, and then, in the evening, I make these balls of pure heaven: crispy outside, creamy inside. You can fill them with meat and cheese if you'd like, but to elevate them from street food and make them part of my summertime menu, I stuff them with crab (or even lobster if I want to be überfancy). These are rich, so allow two or three per serving.

YIELD:
MAKES ABOUT 30 BALLS

SERVE WITH:
GRAPPA-POACHED PEARS WITH SPECK PARMIGIANO-REGGIANO AND PROSCIUTTO SPICED PRUNES

2 tablespoons extra-virgin olive oil

2 tablespoons (¼ stick) unsalted butter, at room temperature

2 shallots, chopped

1 garlic clove, chopped

1 teaspoon kosher salt

1 cup Arborio rice

1 cup dry white wine

2 cups seafood broth or bottled clam juice

½ cup freshly grated Parmigiano-Reggiano

2 tablespoons mascarpone cheese, at room temperature

1 teaspoon grated lemon zest

2 cups lump crabmeat, picked through for shells

2 tablespoons chopped fresh chives

½ cup all-purpose flour

2 large eggs at room temperature, lightly beaten

1 cup panko bread crumbs

Vegetable oil, for frying

1 cup prepared marinara sauce, for dipping (optional)

Heat a 3½-quart Dutch oven over medium-high heat. Add the olive oil and butter, and heat until the butter is melted. To the hot oil, add the shallots and garlic. Cook, stirring often, with a wooden spoon, for about 2 minutes, or until the vegetables are soft and become fragrant. Add ½ teaspoon of the salt to the pan along with the Arborio rice. Stir the rice to coat it with all the flavors of the pan and cook for 1 minute. Stir in the wine, scraping the bottom of the pan, and reduce the heat to medium. Simmer until the wine is almost entirely absorbed, about 3 minutes, stirring frequently. Add all of the broth to the pan and stir to combine. Cook, stirring often, until the rice is tender but not mushy, 15 to 20 minutes. Remove from the heat and stir in the cheeses, lemon zest, crabmeat, and

recipe continues »

chives. Spread the risotto out onto a parchment-lined baking sheet to cool to room temperature. Cover with plastic wrap and refrigerate until completely cold, about 2 hours.

Prepare a breading station using three shallow bowls. Place the flour mixed with the remaining ½ teaspoon salt in one, the eggs in another, and the panko in yet another. Scoop out 1 tablespoon of risotto and, using your palms, shape it into a ball. Roll the ball in the flour mixture, shaking off the excess, then the egg. Lastly dip the ball in the panko, being careful to coat it completely. Place the ball on a rimmed baking sheet. Continue making and coating balls until all the risotto is used.

Fill a medium saucepan with 2 inches of vegetable oil and heat it to 350°F on a deep-fry thermometer over medium-high heat. Using a wire skimmer or a slotted spoon, lower 5 or 6 balls into the oil. Fry for 3 to 4 minutes, or until they are a deep golden brown and heated through. Remove to a paper towel–lined tray. Continue with the rest of the balls, making sure you don't overcrowd the pan to ensure they brown evenly. Serve with warm marinara for dipping, if desired.

ham and ricotta pinwheels

These look really pretty on an antipasto platter, but Jade loves it when I put them in her lunch box, too. For this, you really want to use sturdy slices of Italian cooked ham, not prosciutto, which is too delicate and likely to rip apart when you spread it with the soft ricotta. Jarred giardiniera gives these simple bites a bit of tangy zip.

YIELD:
MAKES 6 ROLLS; SERVES 6 TO 8

SERVE WITH:
AVOCADO WHITE BEAN DIP
CRAB ARANCINI

In a medium bowl, mix together the ricotta, rosemary, Parmigiano-Reggiano, and olive oil with a rubber spatula until well combined. Set aside.

Lay 2 pieces of ham lengthwise on the board in front of you, overlapping them by half and patching holes where needed. Spread about 2 tablespoons of the cheese mixture evenly over the ham. Sprinkle the side closest to you with 2 tablespoons chopped giardiniera and press it gently into the cheese. Roll the ham into a pinwheel, starting with the edge closest to you and rolling away from you. Wrap each roll tightly in plastic wrap and store in the refrigerator for at least 4 hours to firm up. To serve, unwrap the rolls and use a sharp knife to cut each one into ¾-inch pieces.

⅔ cup whole-milk ricotta, at room temperature

¼ teaspoon chopped fresh rosemary

¼ cup freshly grated Parmigiano-Reggiano

2 teaspoons extra-virgin olive oil

12 thin slices Italian cooked ham (prosciutto cotto), about ½ pound

1 cup giardiniera, drained and chopped

SPICY SAUSAGE AND
ESCAROLE SOUP

FLORENTINE
PROSCIUTTO BROTH

TORTELLINI IN
PARMIGIANO-REGGIANO
BRODO

PAPPA AL POMODORO

SIMPLE STRACCIATELLA

ROMAN SEAFOOD
CHOWDER

CAULIFLOWER SOUP
WITH SPICY SALAMI

FARRO AND WHITE BEAN
MINESTRONE

PANE POMODORO

SARDINIAN PASTA SALAD

CALAMARI PANZANELLA

MARINATED SALUMI
SANDWICH

GRILLED CHICKEN AND
BROCCOLI PESTO PANINI

SICILIAN TUNA SALAD
SANDWICH

lunch

When I was growing up, lunch was always a lighter meal than dinner, and very often it was soup. In fact, if I had to name the quintessential Italian lunch, it would probably be *pappa al pomodoro*, a homey, hearty bread-and-tomato soup that is comfort in a bowl. Like most Italians, I love soup. It's warming and sustaining in the way a plate of good pasta is, and making soup is a great means to use up odds and ends you have in the pantry or fridge. I'm not talking about recycling leftovers necessarily, but rather using that last carrot and handful of dried beans or a bit of stale bread and the rind of Parmigiano-Reggiano you've been saving to make something brand-new. Add a green salad and you have a great lunch to take to work—or even a light dinner. If a somewhat heartier salad or a sandwich is more your lunchtime speed, or if you're looking for something to pack along on a picnic, you'll find great options here, too.

spicy sausage and escarole soup

YIELD:
SERVES 6

SERVE WITH:
FULL-BODIED RED WINE

You will find versions of this soup all over Italy, but especially in Tuscany, where sausage and escarole is a classic combination in pasta dishes like orecchiette with sausage and greens. As a soup, it's a perfect one-pot meal. Dipping a hunk of crusty bread in the savory broth is my favorite way to enjoy it.

2 tablespoons extra-virgin olive oil, plus more for drizzling

¾ pound spicy Italian sausage, casings removed

2 shallots, diced

2 carrots, peeled and cut into ⅓-inch pieces

1 celery stalk, cut into ⅓-inch pieces

1 garlic clove, smashed and peeled

¼ teaspoon crushed red pepper flakes

1½ teaspoons kosher salt

4 cups low-sodium chicken broth

1 bay leaf

1 (3-inch) piece of Parmigiano-Reggiano rind

1 small head escarole, chopped into 2-inch pieces

½ pound fresh cheese tortellini, preferably tricolored

Freshly grated Parmigiano-Reggiano, for serving

Heat a 4-quart Dutch oven over medium-high heat. Add the 2 tablespoons of olive oil and heat an additional 10 seconds. Add the sausage to the pan and cook, breaking apart the sausage with the back of a wooden spoon, until it is completely cooked and no pink remains, about 4 minutes.

Add the shallots, carrots, celery, garlic, and red pepper flakes to the pan. Season with the salt and cook, stirring often, for about 4 minutes, or until the shallots are soft. Add 2 cups of water, then add the chicken broth, bay leaf, and cheese rind. Bring to a boil. Reduce the heat to medium-low to maintain a gentle simmer and cook for 5 minutes. Stir in the escarole and tortellini, and return to a simmer. Cook until the pasta is al dente and the escarole is wilted, about 5 minutes. Remove the cheese rind.

Serve sprinkled with freshly grated Parmigiano-Reggiano and a drizzle of extra-virgin olive oil.

florentine prosciutto broth

YIELD:
SERVES 4

SERVE WITH:
**SIMPLE FRISÉE AND ENDIVE
SALAD WITH LEMON
VINAIGRETTE**

The base of this hearty soup is a rich broth flavored with prosciutto and Parmigiano-Reggiano. Because both of these ingredients are quite expensive, practical cooks save all the scraps and end pieces for the soup pot rather than let them go to waste. The result is a really savory broth that can be used in place of chicken broth in soups, stews, and other dishes. Farro and spinach turn it into a meal.

2 carrots, scrubbed and coarsely chopped

2 celery stalks, coarsely chopped

2 shallots, halved

2 garlic cloves, smashed and peeled

5 fresh thyme sprigs

1 ½-inch-thick slice prosciutto di Parma (about ½ pound)

1 (4-inch) piece of Parmigiano-Reggiano rind

½ cup pearled farro, rinsed and drained

1 teaspoon kosher salt

3 tablespoons olive oil

2 onions, sliced into thin half-moons

¼ cup sweet Marsala wine

3 cups chopped baby spinach

4 Parmigiano-Reggiano crisps, for serving (see Cook's Note)

In a Dutch oven or large heavy pot, combine the carrots, celery, shallots, garlic, thyme, prosciutto, and cheese rind. Cover with 7 cups of water and bring to a simmer over medium-low heat. Simmer for 45 minutes, skimming off any foam that rises to the surface. Strain the broth, discarding the solids, and set it aside.

Meanwhile, in a small saucepan, combine the farro with enough water to cover it by an inch. Add the salt and bring to a simmer over medium heat. Cover and simmer for about 20 minutes, or until the farro is tender and most of the water has been absorbed. Drain off any remaining water and set the farro aside.

In a separate Dutch oven or large saucepan, warm the olive oil over medium-high heat. Add the onions and reduce the heat to medium. Cook, stirring often, until deep golden brown, 4 to 5 minutes. Add the Marsala and cook for a minute, stirring the bottom with a wooden spoon to scrape up any brown bits. Add the cooked farro and the broth, and bring to a simmer. Stir in the spinach and cook just until wilted, 30 seconds or so. Serve the soup in bowls topped with a Parmigiano-Reggiano crisp, if you like.

COOK'S NOTE: To make your own Parmigiano-Reggiano crisps, mound heaping tablespoons of grated Parmesan onto a silicone- or parchment-lined baking sheet, spacing them about ½ inch apart. Lightly pat down the mounds. Bake at 400°F for 3 to 5 minutes, or until golden and crisp. Cool on the baking sheet.

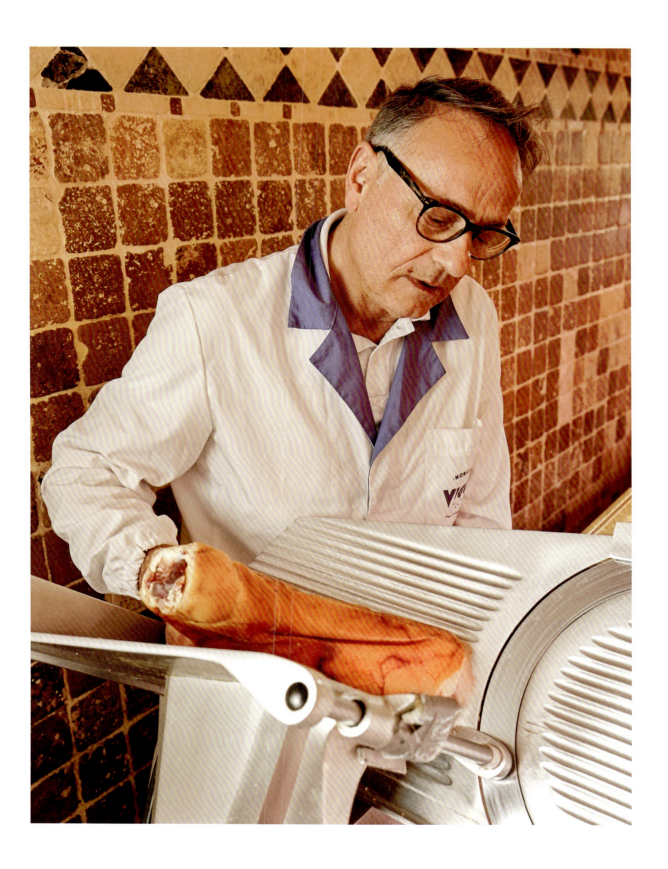

tortellini in parmigiano-reggiano brodo

This dish is all about the Parmigiano-Reggiano, so the quality of the cheese you use really matters here. The better the quality, the more flavorful the broth. In the north of Italy, this is traditionally served at Christmas dinner, but it shouldn't be reserved for the holidays; it's a lovely simple supper, or something to serve instead of chicken soup. It's a great broth for vegetarians, because it has a hearty, meaty flavor without the meat. You can use any kind of pasta you like in place of the tortellini.

1 carrot, peeled and chopped

1 onion, halved

1 head garlic, halved across the equator

1 celery stalk, chopped

4 fresh oregano sprigs

2 fresh thyme sprigs

1 bay leaf

1 pound Parmigiano-Reggiano rinds

1 teaspoon kosher salt, plus more as needed

1 pound cheese tortellini, preferably made with spinach pasta

2 tablespoons chopped fresh flat-leaf parsley

In a large saucepan, combine the carrot, onion, garlic, celery, oregano, thyme, bay leaf, cheese rinds, salt, and 8 cups of water. Place over medium heat and bring to a simmer. Reduce the heat to maintain a simmer and cook the broth gently for 1 hour and 15 minutes, stirring occasionally to prevent the rinds from sticking to the bottom of the pan. Strain the broth into a clean pan and keep it warm over low heat. Discard the solids (I usually snack on the rinds as I cook).

Meanwhile, bring a large pot of salted water to a boil. Cook the tortellini 2 minutes less than the package directions, about 4 minutes. Drain well and add to the broth to finish cooking them. Stir in the parsley and serve.

pappa al pomodoro

When I was growing up, if my mom was in a pinch to get dinner on the table fast, this soup was her go-to. We always had stale bread to use up, and it gives the soup both extra body and a soft, almost silky texture. It's a tasty and hearty lunch that also makes a good weeknight meal.

YIELD:
SERVES 4 TO 6

SERVE WITH:
GRILLED SCALLOPS WITH PROSCIUTTO AND BASIL

MAKE THE SOUP: Heat a medium Dutch oven over medium-high heat. Add the olive oil and pancetta to the pot, and cook until brown and crispy, about 4 minutes. Remove the pancetta to a paper towel–lined plate to drain. Add the onion, carrot, garlic, and red pepper flakes to the pan with the drippings. Reduce the heat to medium and cook, stirring often, for 1 minute, or until fragrant. Add the salt, tomatoes, chicken broth, and bread, and stir to combine. Nestle the basil sprigs and cheese rind in the mixture and bring to a simmer.

Reduce the heat to maintain a gentle bubble. Stir in the drained pancetta. Cook for 25 minutes, stirring often to help break apart the bread and prevent the Parm rind from sticking to the bottom of the pot. Add up to an extra cup of broth, as needed, if the soup gets too thick. Remove and discard the onion, carrot, and cheese rind. Stir in 1 cup of the grated Parmigiano-Reggiano.

TO SERVE, ladle the soup into bowls and garnish with a sprinkling of Parmigiano-Reggiano, a drizzle of extra-virgin olive oil, and the chopped basil.

FOR THE SOUP

2 tablespoons olive oil

4 ounces pancetta, diced

1 small red onion, peeled

1 carrot, peeled and halved

2 garlic cloves, smashed and peeled

¼ teaspoon crushed red pepper flakes

¾ teaspoon kosher salt

2 (14-ounce) cans crushed tomatoes

2 cups low-sodium chicken or vegetable broth, plus up to 1 cup more, if needed

4 cups (1-inch) stale bread cubes (about 2 thick slices)

2 fresh basil sprigs

1 (2-inch) piece of Parmigiano-Reggiano rind

1¼ cups freshly grated Parmigiano-Reggiano

3 tablespoons extra-virgin olive oil

2 tablespoons chopped basil, for garnish

simple stracciatella

The beauty of this soup is its simplicity, because it is mild yet flavorful. It's what my mom would make for my brother, my sister, and me when we were under the weather. It's so soothing and comforting, like a big hug. It's also great for breakfast!

YIELD:
SERVES 4

SERVE WITH:
PANE POMODORO *OR* **MORTADELLA PIADINA**

In a medium bowl, whisk together the bread crumbs, eggs, and ¼ teaspoon of the salt. Set aside.

In a large saucepan, combine the broth, thyme, garlic, and the remaining ¾ teaspoon salt with 2 cups of water. Bring to a simmer over medium heat and cook gently for 5 minutes. Remove the thyme and garlic clove with a slotted spoon and discard. With the broth at a gentle simmer, whisk in the Parmigiano-Reggiano. When the cheese has melted, stir the liquid so that it swirls.

Pour the egg mixture into the center of the swirling liquid and let it cook for 30 seconds, then give it a stir with a fork to break it up a bit. Ladle the soup into bowls and serve garnished with the basil.

¼ cup fine bread crumbs

3 large eggs

½ teaspoon kosher salt

4 cups low-sodium chicken broth

6 fresh thyme sprigs

1 garlic clove, smashed and peeled

1 cup freshly grated Parmigiano-Reggiano

¼ cup chopped fresh basil, for garnish

roman seafood chowder

You will find fish soups in Genoa, Venice, Sicily, and all along the Mediterranean coast of Italy, although most are tomato based. I think this light, herby broth allows you to taste the delicate seafood better. The potatoes are a nod to the soups of Rome, and they give the soup body, something like an American chowder. You could add clams, mussels, calamari, or any other fish you like, but this simple combination of mild fish and shrimp seems to appeal to just about everyone.

YIELD:
SERVES 4

SERVE WITH:
AVOCADO WHITE BEAN DIP ON CROSTINI

In a blender, combine the basil, mint, parsley, chile, ¼ teaspoon of the salt, and ½ cup of the seafood stock. Puree on high until smooth, about 1 minute. Set aside.

Heat the olive oil in a medium Dutch oven over medium heat. When it's hot, add the onion, carrot, celery, and the remaining ½ teaspoon salt to the pot. Cook, stirring often, for 3 minutes. Add the potatoes, the remaining 1½ cups seafood stock, and 1 cup of water. Bring to a simmer and cook gently for 10 minutes, or until the potatoes are tender.

Stir in the shrimp and halibut. Poach for about 5 minutes, or until the shrimp and halibut are cooked through and opaque. Reduce the heat to low, stir in the herb puree, and heat for 1 minute to warm it through. Do not boil. Ladle the soup into serving bowls and sprinkle each serving with the quartered cherry tomatoes. Garnish with more herbs, if desired.

¾ cup packed fresh basil leaves, plus more as needed

¼ cup packed fresh mint leaves, plus more as needed

½ cup packed fresh flat-leaf parsley leaves, plus more as needed

1 fresh serrano chile, stem removed

¾ teaspoon kosher salt

2 cups seafood stock

2 tablespoons olive oil

1 onion, diced

1 carrot, peeled and diced

1 celery stalk, diced

2 large Yukon Gold potatoes (about 12 ounces), peeled and diced

½ pound large shrimp, peeled and deveined

¾ pound halibut, cut into 1½-inch dice

½ cup cherry tomatoes, quartered

cauliflower soup with spicy salami

YIELD:
SERVES 6

SERVE WITH:
HAZELNUT CHICKEN *OR*
**MARINATED BISTECCA
FIORENTINA**

The secret to this soup's velvety texture is—surprise—white chocolate. It's not as strange as it seems; white chocolate is used in northern Italy to finish dishes and give them a velvety sheen. The contrast of the rustic, sharp salami and the rich, faintly sweet veggies and chocolate is really sophisticated and so yummy! Small bowls of this make a nice starter for an elegant meal, but it's also nice right out of a mug on a cold day.

¼ cup olive oil

2 leeks, white parts cleaned and chopped

1 celery stalk, chopped

1 parsnip, peeled and chopped

2½ teaspoons kosher salt

1 head cauliflower, cut into small florets (about 1 pound after trimming)

3 cups low-sodium chicken broth

3 fresh thyme sprigs

1 (2-inch) piece of Parmigiano-Reggiano rind

⅓ cup chopped white chocolate

2 teaspoons fresh lemon juice

2 ounces spicy salami, cut in ¼-inch dice

Extra-virgin olive oil, for drizzling

Heat a large Dutch oven over medium heat. Combine 2 tablespoons of the olive oil, the leeks, celery, and parsnip in the hot pan. Season with 1¼ teaspoons of the salt. Cook, stirring often, for 4 minutes, or until the vegetables are beginning to soften. Add the cauliflower and stir to combine. Add 2 cups of water, then stir in the remaining 1¼ teaspoons salt, the chicken broth, thyme, and cheese rind. Bring to a boil, stirring often. Reduce the heat to low and simmer for 20 minutes, or until the cauliflower and other vegetables are cooked through and soft. Remove from the heat.

Remove the thyme sprigs and cheese rind from the soup and discard. Using an immersion blender, puree the soup until smooth and silky. Return the soup to low heat, add the chocolate, and whisk until it is melted and incorporated into the soup. Stir in the lemon juice. Keep warm.

Heat a small skillet over medium-high heat. Add the remaining 2 tablespoons oil and the diced salami, and cook for about 4 minutes, stirring often, until the salami is evenly browned and crispy. Use a slotted spoon to transfer the salami to a paper towel–lined plate to drain.

To serve, ladle some soup into a bowl. Garnish with a sprinkling of the crispy salami and a drizzle of olive oil.

farro and white bean minestrone

I love minestrone, but I don't love the way the pasta in it always gets soggy. That's why I use farro instead—it adds a nutty flavor and great chewy texture. You could also use barley or brown rice in place of the farro. This is a hearty dish, yet surprisingly light and colorful.

YIELD:
SERVES 4 TO 6

SERVE WITH:
LEMON WHITE PIZZA

Heat a large Dutch oven over medium heat. Add the olive oil and continue to heat until hot. Add the onion, carrots, celery, and ½ teaspoon of the salt. Cook, stirring often with a wooden spoon, for 4 minutes, or until the onions are beginning to soften.

Add the farro and stir, combining it with the vegetables and coating it in the oil. Add 2 cups of water, then stir in the broth, bay leaf, cheese rind, and the remaining ½ teaspoon salt. Bring to a boil, then reduce the heat to medium-low and simmer for 12 minutes.

Stir in the tomatoes and white beans, and continue to simmer for an additional 15 minutes. Remove and discard the bay leaf and rind.

Remove from the heat and stir in the basil and lemon juice. Ladle the soup into serving bowls, drizzle with olive oil, and sprinkle with Parmigiano-Reggiano just before serving.

2 tablespoons extra-virgin olive oil, plus more for drizzling

½ large onion, diced

2 carrots, peeled and cut into ½-inch pieces

1 celery stalk, cut into ½-inch pieces

1 teaspoon kosher salt

1 cup pearled farro, rinsed and drained well

4 cups low-sodium chicken broth

1 bay leaf

1 (4-inch) piece of Parmigiano-Reggiano rind

1 (14-ounce) jar or can cherry tomatoes, drained

1 (15-ounce) can small white beans, such as cannellini, drained and rinsed

¼ cup chopped fresh basil

1½ teaspoons fresh lemon juice

¾ cup freshly grated Parmigiano-Reggiano

pane pomodoro

YIELD:
SERVES 6

SERVE WITH:
**SPICY SAUSAGE AND
ESCAROLE SOUP**

Anything rubbed on hot grilled bread is delicious, but nothing beats ripe, juicy summer tomatoes. The sweet tomato is enhanced by the hot bread. Stack these high on a platter and offer them instead of plain bread for an alfresco lunch with soup or a salad. You can also make this on an outdoor barbecue grill.

6 (1-inch) slices of rustic Italian bread

¼ cup extra-virgin olive oil, plus more for drizzling

1 medium ripe tomato, halved

Pinch of kosher salt

Preheat a grill pan over medium-high heat.

Brush both sides of the bread slices with the olive oil and grill for 3 minutes per side, or until golden brown and toasted. Rub both sides of the grilled bread with the cut side of the tomato, sprinkle with salt, and drizzle with extra oil, if desired.

sardinian pasta salad

YIELD:
SERVES 4

SERVE WITH:
SPICY CALABRIAN SHRIMP

Even if you aren't a fan of pasta salad, this hearty lunch bowl with plenty of veggies will change your mind. It's full of lots of fresh, crunchy beans, herbs, and tomatoes, and a touch of decadent, creamy burrata puts it over the top. *Fregola* is a small Italian pasta from Sardinia; it looks similar to Israeli or pearl couscous, which is a decent substitute if fregola is hard to come by. You'll have extra dressing left over; use it with any kind of warm or cold salad or vegetable dish. It will keep for up to five days, tightly covered, in the refrigerator.

FOR THE DRESSING

3 large shallots

1 cup extra-virgin olive oil

1 cup vegetable oil

¼ cup apple cider vinegar

1 teaspoon Dijon mustard

½ teaspoon kosher salt

FOR THE SALAD

Kosher salt

¼ pound green beans, trimmed and cut into 1-inch pieces

¼ pound wax beans, trimmed and cut into 1-inch pieces

½ cup fregola or Israeli couscous

½ cup frozen shelled edamame, thawed

1 cup cherry tomatoes, quartered

2 tablespoons fresh tarragon leaves, chopped

2 tablespoons fresh basil leaves, chopped

1 pound fresh burrata (2 whole balls), each cut in half

Flake salt, such as Maldon

MAKE THE DRESSING: Place the shallots, olive oil, and vegetable oil in a small saucepan over low heat. Cook the shallots gently for 25 minutes, or until they are completely soft all the way through. Remove from the heat and allow them to cool to room temperature.

Place the softened shallots, ½ cup of the oil, the vinegar, mustard, and salt in a small food processor. Pulse until the shallots are finely chopped and the dressing is thick. Set aside.

PREPARE THE SALAD: Bring a saucepan of salted water to a boil. Fill a bowl with water and ice, and set it aside. Add the green and wax beans to the boiling water and blanch until their color is bright and they are just losing their raw flavor, about 3 minutes. Drain and cool in the ice water.

Bring another saucepan of salted water to a boil. Add the fregola to the boiling water and cook for 8 to 10 minutes, or until it is cooked through. Drain well and place in a large bowl. Add ⅓ cup of the dressing to the bowl and toss to coat. Allow the fregola to cool slightly. Drain the beans and add to the fregola along with the edamame, cherry tomatoes, tarragon, basil, and ½ teaspoon kosher salt; toss gently to coat. Divide the salad among 4 plates and serve topped with a burrata half and sprinkled with flake salt.

calamari panzanella

YIELD:
SERVES 4

SERVE WITH:
CHIANTI AFFOGATO

What's great about this panzanella is that it's a complete meal (greens, protein, bread, and veggies) with lots of flavor, and it's super colorful, all of which makes it a perfect one-dish recipe for entertaining. In Italy, we make it with octopus, but at home it's easier to make with squid. If you're not a fan of the tentacles, just use rings. I like the textural difference, but it's a personal preference.

1 pound cleaned calamari

6 tablespoons olive oil

2 garlic cloves, smashed and peeled

½ teaspoon plus ⅛ teaspoon kosher salt

¼ teaspoon crushed red pepper flakes

2½ tablespoons fresh lemon juice

4 cups (1-inch) stale bread cubes (about 2 thick slices)

½ cup freshly grated Parmigiano-Reggiano

2 cups cherry tomatoes, halved

½ cup pitted kalamata olives, halved

3 cups baby arugula

½ cup fresh basil leaves

⅓ cup extra-virgin olive oil

Rinse the calamari, making sure the bodies are cleaned and the cartilage is removed. Pat dry with paper towels. Slice the bodies into ½-inch rings and leave the tentacles intact.

Heat 2 tablespoons of the olive oil in a large skillet over medium-high heat until a whisper of smoke comes off the pan. Add the garlic and cook for just 30 seconds. Add the calamari, ¼ teaspoon of the salt, and the red pepper flakes to the skillet. Cook, stirring often, for 1 to 2 minutes, or until the calamari is opaque. Be careful not to overcook it. Using a slotted spoon, remove the calamari to a plate and drizzle with 1 tablespoon of the lemon juice.

Preheat the oven to 400°F.

In a medium bowl, combine the bread cubes, the remaining 4 tablespoons olive oil, ¼ teaspoon kosher salt, and the Parmigiano-Reggiano; mix well to coat. Scatter the cubes on a rimmed baking sheet and bake for about 12 minutes, or until golden brown and crispy. Return the toasted cubes to the bowl and add the tomatoes, olives, and arugula.

Tear the basil into small pieces and add it to the bowl. Drizzle the remaining 1½ tablespoons lemon juice and the extra-virgin olive oil around the edge of the bowl and toss well to marry all the ingredients. Add the calamari to the salad along with the remaining ⅛ teaspoon salt. Toss once more and serve.

marinated salumi sandwich

I'm always coming up with versions of the muffuletta sandwich, because they are always a hit, especially good for a picnic or at the beach. They're so full of meat and cheese and veggies that you don't need to serve anything else with them. Best of all, you can make these in advance, and they only get better the longer they sit. I love this basil-almond pesto, and sometimes I make extra and spread it on crostini or serve it over chicken or pork. You could even toss it with rice or pasta for a cold salad.

YIELD:
SERVES 6 TO 8

SERVE WITH:
ITALIAN CARROT SALAD

FOR THE PESTO

½ cup raw almonds

1 small garlic clove

1½ cups fresh basil leaves

1 teaspoon grated lemon zest

¼ cup freshly grated Parmigiano-Reggiano

½ cup extra-virgin olive oil

½ teaspoon kosher salt

FOR THE SANDWICH

1 large loaf ciabatta bread, sliced in half horizontally

¼ pound thinly sliced hot coppa or other spicy salami

¼ pound thinly sliced finocchiona (fennel-flavored salami) or other mild salami

12 ounces lightly salted fresh mozzarella cheese, sliced or torn

2 cups baby arugula

1 small fennel bulb, stalks removed, thinly sliced

1½ tablespoons fresh lemon juice

1 tablespoon extra-virgin olive oil

MAKE THE PESTO: Combine the almonds and garlic in the bowl of a food processor, and pulse to chop coarsely. Add the basil, lemon zest, and Parmigiano-Reggiano, and pulse to combine. Add the olive oil and salt, and puree to a smooth paste.

MAKE THE SANDWICH: Pull out some of the inner bread from the halved loaf, leaving a slightly hollowed shell of crust (see Cook's Note). Spread the pesto evenly over the interior of both sides. Layer the coppa, finocchiona, and mozzarella onto the bottom half. In a small bowl, toss together the arugula, fennel, lemon juice, and olive oil; arrange the mixture on top of the meat and cheese. Top with the remaining bread half, press the sandwich together, and wrap tightly in plastic wrap. Refrigerate for at least an hour or up to overnight before slicing and serving.

COOK'S NOTE: The soft bread pulled from the center of the loaf can be made into bread crumbs and dried for later use. Either pull the bread into bits by hand or whir it briefly in the food processor to get irregular, rustic crumbs. Toast or dry them on a baking sheet and store at room temperature in an airtight container for a month or two.

grilled chicken and broccoli pesto panini

MAKES:
4 SANDWICHES

SERVE WITH:
**CHOCOLATE CHERRY
SHORTBREAD COOKIES**

Not many kids would be excited to find a container of steamed broccoli in their lunch box, but when I make a broccoli pesto and smear it on bread for a sandwich, Jade gobbles it up. It's really nice to be able to use ingredients in unexpected ways so everyone, including me, doesn't get bored. This makes for a wonderful lunch or even dinner when you're on the go! Extra pesto can be stored in the refrigerator in an airtight container for up to four days.

FOR THE PESTO

Kosher salt

2 small heads broccoli, cut in florets (about 3 cups)

1 garlic clove, peeled

1 cup walnuts, toasted (see Cook's Note)

1 tablespoon honey

1 teaspoon grated lemon zest

1 tablespoon fresh lemon juice

1 cup extra-virgin olive oil

½ cup freshly grated Parmigiano-Reggiano

FOR THE SANDWICHES

8 slices rustic bread

4 chicken cutlets

½ teaspoon kosher salt

¼ teaspoon crushed red pepper flakes

1 tablespoon extra-virgin olive oil

1 teaspoon fresh lemon juice

1 or 2 large beefsteak tomatoes, sliced into thick rounds and halved

MAKE THE PESTO: Fill a bowl with ice water. Bring a medium pot of salted water to a boil over medium-high heat. Add the broccoli and cook until tender, about 4 minutes. Use a strainer or a slotted spoon to transfer the cooked broccoli to the ice bath and let it cool, about 3 minutes. Drain the broccoli well, then transfer it to a food processor. Add the garlic, walnuts, honey, ½ teaspoon salt, the lemon zest, and lemon juice, and process until finely chopped. With the machine running, gradually pour in the olive oil. Transfer the pesto to a small bowl and stir in the Parmigiano-Reggiano. Cover and set aside.

MAKE THE SANDWICHES: Preheat a stovetop grill pan over medium-high heat.

Grill the slices of bread until toasted and golden brown, about 2 minutes per side. Season the chicken cutlets with the salt and red pepper flakes, and drizzle with the olive oil. Grill the cutlets until they are golden brown and cooked through, 3 to 4 minutes per side. Squeeze the lemon juice over the cooked chicken while still on the grill, then transfer the chicken to a plate.

TO ASSEMBLE THE SANDWICHES, spread about 1 tablespoon of the pesto on each slice of grilled bread. Place 2 pieces of tomato on 4 of the slices. Top the tomatoes with a chicken cutlet and the remaining slice of bread. Cut each in half and serve.

COOK'S NOTE: To toast walnuts, spread them on a rimmed baking sheet. Place in a preheated 350°F oven for 8 to 10 minutes, stirring once or twice, until they are fragrant and lightly browned. Transfer to a bowl or cutting board to cool completely.

sicilian tuna salad sandwich

YIELD:
MAKES 6 OPEN-FACE
SANDWICHES

SERVE WITH:
ANTIPASTI IN A JAR
SALTED DARK CHOCOLATE
CHUNK BROWNIES

This is inspired by the sandwiches my family always brought along for picnics at the beach, while hiking, or just sitting by the pool. The crisp English muffin makes the sandwich so much lighter—and so easy to eat. A creamy white bean spread made with mascarpone cheese acts as a mayo substitute; it's the perfect counterpoint to the zesty tuna mixture, but you could also use it as a dip for veggies or as a pita filling with grilled fish, chicken, or veggies.

FOR THE WHITE BEAN SPREAD

1 (15-ounce) can cannellini beans, drained and rinsed

8 ounces mascarpone cheese, at room temperature

1 teaspoon kosher salt

1 tablespoon grated lemon zest

2 tablespoons freshly squeezed lemon juice

1 tablespoon extra-virgin olive oil

FOR THE TUNA SALAD

1 (6.7-ounce) jar olive-oil packed tuna, drained and flaked

2 celery stalks with leaves, finely chopped

2 tablespoons finely chopped sun-dried tomatoes packed in oil

1 tablespoon capers, drained and rinsed

1 tablespoon fresh flat-leaf parsley, chopped

2 tablespoons extra-virgin olive oil

1 tablespoon fresh lemon juice

½ teaspoon kosher salt

¼ teaspoon freshly ground black pepper

3 English muffins, toasted

¼ cup baby arugula

Extra-virgin olive oil, for drizzling

MAKE THE WHITE BEAN SPREAD: In the bowl of a food processor, combine the beans, mascarpone, salt, and lemon zest, and process for 30 seconds, until pureed. With the machine running, add the lemon juice and olive oil, and continue to process until smooth, about another 30 seconds. Set aside.

MAKE THE TUNA SALAD: In a medium bowl, stir together the tuna, chopped celery stalks and leaves, sun-dried tomatoes, capers, parsley, olive oil, lemon juice, salt, and pepper.

Spread 2 tablespoons of the white bean spread onto each English muffin half. Arrange a few arugula leaves on the spread and top with 2 tablespoons of the tuna salad and a drizzle of olive oil.

In America, pizza is served up in slices, usually as a meal in its own right, but to an Italian, a little bit of pizza or any of the small bites in this chapter would be considered *tramezzini,* which literally translates as "in-betweens." These are more like snacks than legit meals, something to tide you over before a big weekend feast, or between breakfast and lunch or lunch and dinner. Most pair a crust, a toast, or a small piece of bread with a smidge of flavorful topping—just enough to tame your hunger without killing your appetite. That said, any of these snack foods could easily be a lunch or light dinner with a green salad, and most would be a perfect addition to a party buffet or game night. In other words, they work for all those "what should I make?" occasions—and anytime in between!

in-betweens

LEMON WHITE PIZZA

SMOKED SCAMORZA, SPINACH, AND PANCETTA PIZZA

SAUSAGE AND BROCCOLI PIZZA

FENNEL GRATIN PIZZETTE

POSITANO PIZZAS

SAVORY CROSTATA

CROSTINI WITH SMOKED TROUT

BRUSCHETTA WITH BURRATA AND KALE SALSA VERDE

MOZZARELLA AND STRAWBERRY BRUSCHETTA

MORTADELLA PIADINA

TRAMEZZINI (ITALIAN TEA SANDWICHES)

lemon white pizza

YIELD:
SERVES 4 TO 6

SERVE WITH:
ICED AMERICANO

Lemon spaghetti is one of my signature dishes, and this pizza has all the same great flavors in a bite-size finger food. It's a lighter, brighter take on pizza—no red sauce, but lots of ooey-gooey, creamy goodness.

1 (16-ounce) ball of store-bought pizza dough

1 cup whole-milk ricotta

2 teaspoons grated lemon zest

¼ teaspoon kosher salt

½ teaspoon dried oregano

All-purpose flour, for dusting

1 tablespoon olive oil

4 ounces fresh mozzarella cheese, torn into pieces

½ cup freshly grated Parmigiano-Reggiano

¼ cup fresh basil leaves, torn

¼ teaspoon crushed red pepper flakes

Place the pizza dough in a lightly oiled bowl, cover with a towel, and allow it to rest in a warm place for 1 hour.

Position racks in the upper and lower thirds of the oven. Preheat the oven to 450°F.

In a small bowl, combine the ricotta, lemon zest, salt, and oregano. Set aside.

Using a touch of flour to prevent sticking, stretch out the pizza dough to an 11 × 16-inch oval. Turn a rimmed baking sheet upside down and drizzle with the olive oil. Place the dough on the baking sheet. Spread the ricotta mixture evenly over the crust, leaving a ½-inch border around the edge. Divide the mozzarella evenly over the ricotta.

Place the pizza on the lowest rack in the oven and bake for 10 minutes. Rotate the pizza to the upper rack and bake an additional 10 minutes, or until deep golden brown. Remove the pizza to a rack and sprinkle with the Parmigiano-Reggiano, basil, and red pepper flakes. Cut into pieces and serve.

smoked scamorza, spinach, and pancetta pizza

This is one of my favorite combinations, an Italian twist on American breakfast flavors. Smoked scamorza is a southern Italian cheese similar to mozzarella with a woodsy flavor and aroma that I love. Because it's a little drier than mozzarella, it doesn't make the dough soggy, so you get the perfect pizza crust. Serve this for Sunday brunch.

YIELD:
SERVES 4

SERVE WITH:
BLOODY MARY

Place the pizza dough in a lightly oiled bowl, cover with a towel, and allow it to rest in a warm place for 1 hour.

Position one rack in the highest position of the oven and remove the others. Preheat the oven to 500°F.

Place the pancetta in a large skillet and cook over medium-high heat, stirring often with a wooden spoon, until crispy, about 8 minutes. Drain off half of the fat. Add the spinach to the hot pan, turn off the heat, and stir until the spinach is wilted. Set aside.

Dust a rimmed baking sheet that has been flipped upside down with the flour. Gently stretch the pizza dough into a round and place it on the flour-dusted baking sheet. Continue to stretch out to a ¼-inch thickness, leaving it a little thicker around the edges. Sprinkle the dough with half of the cheese. Spoon the spinach mixture over the cheese layer and top with the remaining cheese. Place the baking sheet directly on the floor of the oven and bake for 5 minutes, then move the sheet to the top shelf and finish cooking for an additional 5 minutes, until the crust is golden brown and cooked.

When you move the pizza to the top rack, heat the olive oil in a medium skillet over medium heat. Crack the 4 eggs into the skillet and cook them until the whites are set but the yolks are still runny, about 3 minutes. Slide the eggs onto the pizza and serve.

1 (16-ounce) ball of store-bought pizza dough

4 ounces thinly sliced pancetta, chopped

5 ounces baby spinach, chopped

3 tablespoons all-purpose flour, for dusting

½ pound smoked scamorza or smoked mozzarella cheese, grated

1 tablespoon extra-virgin olive oil

4 large eggs, at room temperature

sausage and broccoli pizza

YIELD:
SERVES 4

SERVE WITH:
CRAB ARANCINI

This kid-friendly combo is one of Jade's favorites. I grew up eating pizza topped with a fresh tomato sauce, not the cooked sauce you usually get at an American pizzeria. This hybrid version falls somewhere in between, with the lighter and sweeter flavor of a fresh sauce but the smooth texture of a cooked one.

FOR THE SAUCE

1 (28-ounce) can tomato puree

½ cup lightly packed fresh basil leaves, torn into pieces

½ cup extra-virgin olive oil

¾ teaspoon kosher salt

FOR THE PIZZA

1 (16-ounce) ball of store-bought pizza dough

2 tablespoons extra-virgin olive oil

1 pound spicy Italian sausage, casings removed

1 bunch broccoli, cut into bite-size florets (about 3 cups)

3 tablespoons all-purpose flour, for dusting

¾ pound fresh mozzarella cheese, cut in ¼-inch slices

1 cup freshly grated Parmigiano-Reggiano

MAKE THE SAUCE: In a medium bowl, combine the tomato puree, basil, olive oil, and salt. Stir together until combined. Cover with plastic wrap and refrigerate for at least 3 hours to allow the flavors to marry.

MAKE THE PIZZA: Place the pizza dough in a lightly oiled bowl, cover with a towel, and allow it to rest in a warm place for 1 hour.

Position one rack in the top third of the oven and remove the others. Preheat the oven to 500°F.

Heat a large skillet over high heat. Add the olive oil and sausage and cook, breaking the sausage into bite-size pieces with a wooden spoon, until the sausage is golden brown and cooked through, about 10 minutes. Add the broccoli to the skillet and stir for a minute or so, then cool to room temperature.

Flip a rimmed baking sheet upside down and sprinkle it with the flour. Gently stretch the pizza dough into a round and place it on the flour-dusted baking sheet. Continue to stretch it out to a ¼-inch thickness, leaving it a little thicker around the edges. Spread 1 cup of the sauce over the dough and top it with the mozzarella. Top with the sausage mixture and the grated Parmigianio-Reggiano.

Bake the pizza directly on the oven floor for 5 minutes, then move it to the top rack for an additional 5 minutes, or until golden brown.

fennel gratin pizzette

YIELD:
MAKES 4 PIZZETTES

SERVE WITH:
CAMPARI AND SODA

I used to make pizza with my brother Dino on Sundays, when we would invite friends and family over for dinner. This was always our appetizer. Ricotta and mozzarella make a pillowy bed for the veggie topping, which gets a nice licorice flavor from the fennel. With the sweet tomatoes, it's almost like an Italian spring salad on a pizza. One of my favorites!

1 (16-ounce) ball of store-bought pizza dough

1 small fennel bulb

All-purpose flour, for dusting

¼ cup extra-virgin olive oil

1 cup whole-milk ricotta

8 ounces fresh mozzarella cheese, torn into small pieces

1 cup cherry tomatoes, sliced or quartered

½ teaspoon kosher salt

1 cup freshly grated Parmigiano-Reggiano

Place the pizza dough in a lightly oiled bowl, cover with a towel, and allow it to rest in a warm place for 1 hour.

Position racks in the upper and lower thirds of the oven. Preheat the oven to 450°F.

Separate the stalks from the fennel bulb and reserve some of the leafy fronds for garnish. Halve and core the bulb, then use a mandoline to slice the fennel as thinly as possible. Set aside.

Divide the rested dough into 4 equal-size pieces. Dust a counter with some flour and roll each piece of dough into a round ¼ inch thick, dusting the dough with flour as needed to prevent sticking. Place 2 dough rounds on each of 2 rimmed baking sheets. Brush the dough with half of the olive oil. Dot each round evenly with the ricotta and the torn mozzarella. Sprinkle with the tomatoes and season with the salt. Top with the fennel and a drizzle of the remaining 2 tablespoons olive oil. Bake for 20 minutes, switching the positions of the baking sheets halfway through.

After 20 minutes, remove the baking sheets from the oven and sprinkle the pizzettes evenly with the Parmigiano-Reggiano. Turn the broiler to high and place one sheet under the broiler for 3 minutes, or until the Parmigiano-Reggiano is melted and browned. Repeat with the remaining sheet. Sprinkle with fennel fronds and serve.

positano pizzas

While spending time in Positano, I was served a version of this dish as an amuse-bouche at a beachside restaurant called Le Tre Sorelle. The pizzas are so much fun to make with Jade and her friends back home, and they are also a great light lunch or snack.

YIELD:
MAKES 6 (5-INCH) HEARTS

SERVE WITH:
ICED TEA OR FLAVORED SELTZER

Place the pizza dough in a lightly oiled bowl, cover with a towel, and allow it to rest in a warm place for 1 hour.

Preheat the oven to 375°F.

Pierce each tomato with the tip of a paring knife. On a small rimmed baking sheet, combine the tomatoes, olive oil, salt, garlic, and basil. Toss to coat and roast for 30 minutes, or until the tomatoes are beginning to blister. Set aside to cool.

Raise the oven temperature to 425°F.

On a lightly floured board, use a rolling pin to roll out the pizza dough to a ¼-inch thickness. Using a cookie cutter or the tip of a sharp knife, cut out six 5-inch hearts and place them on a rimmed baking sheet. Bake the hearts for about 12 minutes, or until lightly puffed and beginning to brown. Remove from the oven and cool slightly. Split the hearts in half horizontally, as if you were making a sandwich. Divide the mozzarella and tomatoes over the bottom halves and sprinkle evenly with the Parmigiano-Reggiano. Replace the tops and brush with extra-virgin olive oil. Sprinkle each heart with oregano.

Bake for 5 minutes, or until the cheese is melted and the tops are golden. Serve warm, drizzled with more extra-virgin olive oil, if desired.

1 (16-ounce) ball of store-bought pizza dough

1 pint cherry tomatoes

3 tablespoons olive oil

½ teaspoon kosher salt

4 garlic cloves, smashed and peeled

2 fresh basil sprigs

All-purpose flour, for dusting

½ cup freshly grated mozzarella cheese

½ cup freshly grated Parmigiano-Reggiano

2 tablespoons extra-virgin olive oil, plus more for drizzling

½ teaspoon dried oregano

pizza geometry

In America pizza generally comes in wedges, triangular pieces cut from a round pie. In Rome, though, many traditional shops bake their pizza in rectangular shapes and sell it by weight, allowing customers to choose how much or little they want. These pies can be up to 3 or 4 feet long, topped with everything from fresh burrata to clouds of thinly sliced prosciutto, potatoes and rosemary, or just a simple fresh tomato sauce, all on a thin, yeasty crust. A regional favorite is fresh zucchini flowers stuffed with anchovies. When you make your selection, the pizzaiola will use a big knife to slice off a section to your specification, toss it on the scale, then fold it in half and hand it over on a piece of wax paper—perfect for munching as you stroll around the city.

savory crostata

I discovered pissaladière, a sweet onion tart baked on a pizza-like crust, when I was a culinary student living in Paris, and it was love at first bite. My version incorporates more vegetables (and omits the traditional anchovies!) and uses a puff pastry crust so it's an anytime snack. It's still one of the best!

YIELD:
SERVES 6 TO 8

SERVE WITH:
CRISP WHITE WINE

Preheat the oven to 375°F.

Unfold the puff pastry and place on a lightly floured surface. Roll out the dough into a 10-inch square. Place a 10-inch ovenproof skillet on top and trace around the bottom with the tip of a paring knife. Cut out the round and refrigerate it until ready to use.

Place the same skillet over medium-high heat. Add the olive oil and onions, and reduce the heat to medium. Cook, stirring often, until the onions are soft, sweet, and dark golden brown. This will take about 15 minutes. Season the onions with the ½ teaspoon salt and stir in the balsamic vinegar. Sprinkle with the oregano and remove from the heat.

Using a rubber spatula, spread the onions evenly over the bottom of the pan. Place the ricotta in a small bowl and season with the remaining ⅛ teaspoon salt and the black pepper. Place 8 to 10 dollops of ricotta over the onions. Using a fork, prick the cold puff pastry a few times, place it over the onions and cheese, and press down gently to make sure the dough is touching the filling. Bake for 35 to 40 minutes, or until the pastry is puffed and golden brown.

Remove the skillet from the oven and carefully place a slightly larger plate over the top. Invert the tart onto the plate, replacing any onions that may have stuck to the pan. Allow the tart to cool slightly.

Meanwhile, in a small bowl, dress the arugula with the lemon juice. Sprinkle the arugula over the top of the semi-cool tart and nestle the tomatoes into the onions. Slice into wedges or squares and serve.

1 sheet (approximately 8 ounces) frozen puff pastry, thawed

All-purpose flour, for dusting

2 tablespoons olive oil

2 large onions, halved lengthwise and thinly sliced

½ teaspoon plus ⅛ teaspoon kosher salt

2 teaspoons balsamic vinegar

1 tablespoon fresh oregano leaves, chopped

½ cup whole-milk ricotta

⅛ teaspoon freshly ground black pepper

¼ cup baby arugula

½ teaspoon freshly squeezed lemon juice

4 cherry tomatoes, halved

coffee break

Italians drink coffee all day long, as evidenced by the stand-up espresso bars on every street where customers can grab a shot, down it, and go on their way. Italians are more likely to have a milky coffee drink like a cappuccino or a latte at breakfast time; after the evening meal a final straight shot of espresso, maybe with a bit of grappa to flavor it—in which case it is called café correcto, or "corrected"—is considered an essential ending to the day. After living in the United States for so long, I've become a convert to the Americano, espresso "stretched" with hot water in the style of American coffee, for my afternoon pick-me-up. But in the summertime my favorite coffee drink is a *shekeratto*, espresso shaken very vigorously with a little sugar and a lot of ice until the liquid is light and frothy, with a foamy head. It's luscious without any dairy and incredibly refreshing on a hot day!

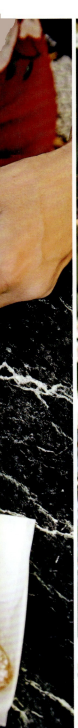

crostini with smoked trout

YIELD:
MAKES 20 CROSTINI

SERVE WITH:
AVOCADO WHITE BEAN DIP AND CRUDITES

When I was a kid, my family ate a lot of *bacala* (salted cod). I will admit it wasn't my favorite, because it was on the bland side and the texture was soft and mushy. My update uses either smoked trout or whitefish (whichever I can find) instead of dried and salted cod, and it adds "everything bagel" seasonings to create a dish that nods to tradition but with a whole lot more flavor and texture. Now it is one of my favorite crostini.

1 teaspoon white sesame seeds

1 teaspoon poppy seeds

½ teaspoon onion powder

½ teaspoon garlic powder

¼ teaspoon kosher salt

½ baguette, cut into 20 (¼-inch) slices

¼ cup extra-virgin olive oil

8 ounces flaked smoked trout or smoked whitefish

2 tablespoons fresh dill, chopped

6 tablespoons crème fraîche

20 caper berries, halved, or 2 tablespoons regular capers, drained and rinsed

Preheat the oven to 350°F.

In a small bowl, mix together the sesame seeds, poppy seeds, onion powder, garlic powder, and salt. Brush each baguette slice on both sides with olive oil and arrange them on a rimmed baking sheet in a single layer. Sprinkle evenly with the seed mixture. Bake for 8 to 10 minutes, or until lightly browned and crisp. Cool to room temperature.

Remove the skin, if any, from the smoked fish and discard. Using your hands or a fork, crumble and flake the fish into a small bowl. Add the dill and crème fraîche, and mix gently with a rubber spatula.

Spread each crostini with a spoonful of the fish salad and top with 2 caper berry halves or a few capers.

bruschetta with burrata and kale salsa verde

My California side comes through loud and clear in this dish that I came up with in Florence. It's full of Tuscan flavors and healthy greens for the best of both worlds. The kale salsa is similar to a pesto but looser, so the bread softens as it absorbs the salsa. Topped with silky burrata, it's perfect with a glass of wine.

YIELD:
SERVES 6

SERVE WITH:
ITALIAN BEER

MAKE THE SALSA: In the bowl of a food processor, pulse together the kale and garlic until coarsely chopped. Add the salt, capers, anchovy paste, mustard, and vinegar, and pulse once or twice more. Add the olive oil and process for 5 seconds. Set aside to let the flavors marry.

Preheat a grill pan over high heat.

Drizzle both halves of the bread evenly with the olive oil. Grill for about 2 minutes on each side, or until golden brown and charred in a few spots. Remove the bread to a cutting board. Spoon the salsa verde evenly over each bread half. Tear the burrata over the salsa verde and scatter the tomatoes and pine nuts evenly over everything. Cut the bread halves into slices and serve.

FOR THE SALSA

1½ cups chopped Tuscan kale (about 8 large leaves), stems removed

1 garlic clove, smashed and peeled

¼ teaspoon plus ⅛ teaspoon kosher salt

3 tablespoons capers, drained and rinsed

1 teaspoon anchovy paste

1 tablespoon Dijon mustard

2 tablespoons apple cider vinegar

½ cup extra-virgin olive oil

1 loaf ciabatta bread, cut in half horizontally

¼ cup extra-virgin olive oil

½ pound fresh burrata or mozzarella cheese (about 2 medium balls)

8 oil-packed sun-dried tomatoes, coarsely chopped

3 tablespoons pine nuts, toasted

mozzarella and strawberry bruschetta

YIELD:
MAKES 15 CROSTINI

SERVE WITH:
ROSE PROSECCO

This bruschetta captures the essence of Capri and the Amalfi coast in a single bite, with the perfect balance of sweet and savory notes. It's one of my favorite things to eat in the summer, when both strawberries and tomatoes taste of the sun.

15 (¼-inch) slices of baguette

2 tablespoons olive oil

½ teaspoon kosher salt

1 tablespoon white balsamic vinegar

2 tablespoons extra-virgin olive oil

1 teaspoon honey, preferably clover honey

½ teaspoon kosher salt

½ cup quartered cherry tomatoes

¾ cup chopped strawberries

1 tablespoon chopped fresh basil

8 ounces fresh mozzarella cheese (1 ball), chilled

Preheat the oven to 400°F.

Brush each baguette slice on both sides with the olive oil and arrange them on a rimmed baking sheet. Sprinkle with the salt and bake for 10 minutes, rotating the baking sheet halfway through if they are not browning evenly.

In a medium bowl, whisk together the vinegar, extra-virgin olive oil, honey, and salt until smooth and emulsified. Add the tomatoes, strawberries, and basil, and mix well to coat. Allow the mixture to sit at room temperature for 10 minutes to let the flavors marry.

Slice the mozzarella into small pieces. Place a slice on each of the crostini and top it with some of the strawberry mixture. Drizzle with a touch of the dressing, if desired.

mortadella piadina

Piadina is a focaccia-like flatbread made from pizza dough that can be filled with any ingredient—just like a tortilla—so think of this as an Italian version of a quesadilla! My mother often made these for an easy weeknight meal, and to this day I *love* mortadella. Warmed, with the prosciutto cotto (cooked ham) and cheese, these flavors take me back to my childhood. You can cut this into narrow wedges as a game-day snack for a big crew, or serve larger portions with a salad for a light lunch.

YIELD:
SERVES 4 TO 6

SERVE WITH:
DRY WHITE WINE

Place the pizza dough in a lightly oiled bowl, cover with a towel, and allow it to rest in a warm place for 1 hour.

Preheat the oven to 425°F.

Drizzle 1 tablespoon of the olive oil on a rimmed baking sheet. Using your hands, stretch the dough to an 11-inch round about ⅓ inch thick. Drizzle another tablespoon of oil over the dough and dimple the top with your fingertips. Sprinkle with the salt and bake for 13 to 15 minutes, or until puffed and golden brown.

Use tongs to transfer the crust to a cutting board, working quickly while the crust is still hot. Split the crust in half horizontally with a serrated knife, using a clean towel to protect your hand if the crust is too hot to handle. Layer the provolone onto the bottom crust, overlapping the slices as needed to fit, followed by the prosciutto cotto and then the mortadella, laying the thin slices with a slight ribbon effect so they are airy, not flattened down.

Sprinkle the arugula over the top and drizzle with the remaining 1 tablespoon olive oil. Replace the top crust and let the piadina sit for 5 minutes so the flavors can marry and the filling softens a bit. Cut into wedges and serve.

1 (16-ounce) ball of store-bought pizza dough

3 tablespoons extra-virgin olive oil

½ teaspoon flake salt, such as Maldon

¼ pound provolone cheese, thinly sliced

½ pound prosciutto cotto, thinly sliced

½ pound mortadella, thinly sliced

1½ cups baby arugula

tramezzini (italian tea sandwiches)

YIELD:
MAKES 16 TEA SANDWICHES

SERVE WITH:
DRY WHITE WINE OR FLAVORED SELTZER

Tramezzini is the Italian term for finger sandwiches, much like the crustless sandwiches you might have with afternoon tea. In Rome you'll see an assortment in most bakeries and snack bars, but at times you'll even see them on a breakfast buffet! To make them a little less filling I make mine open-faced, although that's not traditional. I'm especially fond of the flavors I've suggested here; the toasted quinoa adds a fun crunch to the buttery avocado toast.

PROSCIUTTO AND RICOTTA

4 thin slices white bread

2 tablespoons ricotta

Pinch of salt

½ teaspoon lemon zest

4 thin slices Prosciutto San Danielle

16 leaves baby arugula

OPEN-FACED AVOCADO

2 thin slices whole wheat bread

2 teaspoons toasted quinoa

½ avocado, pitted and mashed

½ teaspoon lemon zest

½ teaspoon lemon juice

⅛ teaspoon red pepper flakes

¼ teaspoon flake salt

SMOKED SALMON

2 tablespoons crème fraîche

2 teaspoons chopped chives

2 teaspoons capers, chopped

4 thin slices white or dark rye bread

2 slices smoked wild salmon

TOMATO AND MOZZARELLA

4 thin slices white or whole wheat bread

2 tablespoons prepared pesto

2 (⅓-inch) slices tomato on the vine, halved

2 (⅓-inch) slices fresh mozzarella cheese, halved

TO MAKE THE PROSCIUTTO AND RICOTTA SANDWICHES: Toast the bread and cut off the crusts. In a small bowl, mix together the ricotta, salt, and lemon zest. Spread the mixture on 2 pieces of the toast. Ribbon 2 pieces of prosciutto on top of each and garnish with the arugula leaves. Top each with a second piece of toast and cut into triangles or rectangles.

TO MAKE THE OPEN-FACED AVOCADO SANDWICHES: Toast the bread and cut off the crusts. Cut each slice diagonally into 2 triangles.

Rinse the quinoa under running water. Heat a small heavy skillet over medium heat. Add the damp quinoa to the pan and cook, stirring often, for 5 to 7 minutes or until the quinoa is dry, lightly browned, and beginning to pop. Cool the quinoa on a plate.

Mix the avocado, lemon zest, lemon juice, and red pepper flakes in a small bowl. Spoon some of the avocado mash on each piece of toast. Sprinkle evenly with salt.

TO MAKE THE SMOKED SALMON SANDWICHES: In a small bowl, mix together the crème fraîche, chives, and capers. Spread the mixture evenly over the bread slices. Ribbon one piece of salmon each on two bread slices. Top with the remaining sauced bread slices. Trim off the crusts, then cut each sandwich diagonally into triangles or lengthwise into fingers.

TO MAKE THE TOMATO AND MOZZARELLA SANDWICHES: Toast the bread and cut off the crusts. Spread the toasts evenly with the pesto. Top 2 of the toasts with a slice of tomato and a slice of mozzarella. Top with the remaining pesto toasts. Cut into triangles or rectangles.

CACIO E PEPE WITH PANCETTA AND ARUGULA

SPICY LINGUINE WITH WALNUTS AND MINT

FUSILLI WITH FRESH POMODORO

LEMON AND PEA ALFREDO

SWEET ONION CARBONARA

PENNE WITH CORN AND SPICY SAUSAGE

ORZO WITH CLAMS

MEZZI RIGATONI WITH BUTTERNUT SQUASH AND SPICY SAUSAGE

BITTER RICE

ITALIAN CHICKEN AND RICE

CRISPY CHICKEN THIGHS WITH PEPPERS AND CAPERS

ITALIAN SHEET-PAN CHICKEN WITH BREAD SALAD

CHICKEN AGRODOLCE

SPICY TURKEY POLPETONE

HERB-ROASTED PORK TENDERLOIN

FLANK STEAK WITH ROASTED GRAPES AND MUSHROOMS

PAN-SEARED BRANZINO WITH TOMATO AND CAPERS

GRILLED SWORDFISH WITH CANDIED LEMON SALAD

SALMON WITH PUTTANESCA

FLOUNDER PICCATA

PAN-SEARED SALMON WITH ARTICHOKES AND WHITE WINE

LEMON SOLE OREGANATA

MONKFISH CACCIATORE

MUSSELS IN WHITE WINE

weeknights

You know the drill. Despite your best intentions to start the week with a big shop and a menu plan, somehow dinnertime always seems to sneak up on you, and suddenly you just need to make dinner fast. Plenty of days when four o'clock rolls around, I find myself racking my brain for something I can make on the fly before Jade gets so ravenous that she fills up on snacks (or worse). It's not so different in Italy, but our weeknight fallbacks in the States—takeout or fast food—aren't quite so ingrained in the culture there. Instead, busy Italian cooks rely on simple pastas and easy seafood and meat dishes that can be produced pronto and without a lot of fuss. These are the dishes I grew up eating, revisited with American supermarkets in mind and made a bit lighter. Because they can't develop flavor through long, slow cooking, they rely on bright, strong notes like those from olives, Calabrian chiles, and tangy ricotta salata cheese, to add a bit of zing to a quickly assembled meal. Many of the sauces— even the pasta sauces—are mix and match, so if there is one your team especially goes for, try it with a different protein to change things up.

cacio e pepe with pancetta and arugula

What makes this dish great is its simplicity. Traditional *cacio e pepe* doesn't include greens, but I find some arugula lightens up the dish. Feel free to swap the arugula for peas or asparagus spears or even artichoke hearts. It's an all-in-one meal, no salad needed! The starchy pasta cooking water is an important element of the recipe, so don't forget to reserve some before you drain the pasta; you can't make the sauce without it! I love how the gooey melted cheese mixes with the pepper and pancetta. This is my friend Shane's favorite dish and I make it for him often.

YIELD:
SERVES 6

SERVE WITH:
A MEDIUM-BODIED RED WINE

Bring a large pot of salted water to a boil over high heat. Add the pasta and cook 2 minutes less than the package directions, about 8 minutes. Drain well, reserving 1½ cups of the pasta cooking water.

Meanwhile, heat a large straight-sided skillet over medium heat. Add the olive oil and pancetta. Cook, stirring often with a wooden spoon, until the pancetta is crisp, about 10 minutes. Add the pepper and toast it, stirring often, for about a minute, or until fragrant. Add ½ cup of the reserved pasta water and scrape up any bits that are sticking to the bottom of the skillet.

Add the pasta and sprinkle with the Parmigiano-Reggiano. Add another ½ cup of the reserved pasta water and stir to coat all of the pasta in the cheese. Add the pecorino and butter, and stir to combine, creating a light, creamy cheese sauce. Add the arugula and cook until wilted. Add additional reserved pasta water as needed to maintain the light sauce consistency. Serve with more grated Parmigiano-Reggiano, if desired.

Kosher salt

1 pound creste di gallo pasta (cock's comb shaped) or other short pasta

2 tablespoons extra-virgin olive oil

⅓ pound pancetta, diced

1½ teaspoons coarsely ground black pepper

2 cups freshly grated Parmigiano-Reggiano, plus more (optional) for serving

1 cup freshly grated pecorino cheese

2 tablespoons (¼ stick) unsalted butter, at room temperature

3 cups packed baby arugula, roughly chopped

spicy linguine with walnuts and mint

YIELD:
SERVES 6

SERVE WITH:
**ENDIVE, PANCETTA, AND
TOMATO SALAD
WHOLE ROASTED FISH**

When you need a pasta you can put together quickly with things from the pantry, this very tasty dish is perfect. It's super fast to make, and although it looks a little plain, it packs lots of flavor from the anchovy paste and spice from the Calabrian chile. It's versatile, too; I like to serve it either as a light supper or as a first course before a whole roasted fish.

Kosher salt

1 pound linguine

1 teaspoon Calabrian chile paste, or more to taste

1 tablespoon anchovy paste

½ cup extra-virgin olive oil

1 cup freshly grated Parmigiano-Reggiano

½ cup walnuts, toasted (see Cook's Note, page 75) and chopped

½ cup fresh mint leaves, roughly chopped or torn

1 cup baby arugula, roughly chopped or torn

Bring a large pot of salted water to a boil over high heat. Add the pasta and cook for 8 to 10 minutes, or until al dente. Drain well, reserving 1 cup of the pasta cooking water.

In a large bowl, whisk together the chile paste, anchovy paste, and olive oil. Add the drained pasta, top with the Parmigiano-Reggiano, and toss well, adding the reserved pasta water, as needed, to create a sauce. Add the walnuts, mint, and arugula, and toss well.

fusilli with fresh pomodoro

Someplace between a raw tomato sauce and one made with canned tomatoes, this quick sauce gets its unique texture from an unusual technique. Grating the tomatoes makes it taste bright and fresh, but it's still meaty.

YIELD:
SERVES 6
SERVE WITH:
ASPARAGUS WITH GRILLED MELON SALAD

Bring a large pot of salted water to a boil over high heat. Add the pasta and cook 2 minutes less than the package directions, about 8 minutes. Drain well, reserving 1 cup of the pasta cooking water.

Using the large holes on a box grater, grate the flesh of the tomatoes until you are left with just the skin. Heat a large straight-sided skillet over medium-high heat and add the olive oil. Once the oil is hot, add the garlic and cook, stirring constantly, until the garlic is fragrant and beginning to brown, about 2 minutes. Add the grated tomatoes, the whole basil sprigs, and ¾ teaspoon salt to the hot oil. Reduce the heat to medium-low and cook for 5 minutes. Remove the garlic and basil sprigs, and stir in the ricotta. Add the pasta, followed by the Parmigiano-Reggiano. Stir to combine and coat everything in the sauce.

Cook for another 2 minutes to finish cooking the pasta and thicken the sauce slightly, adding some of the reserved pasta water if it looks dry. Stir in the chopped basil and serve topped with additional ricotta and Parmigiano-Reggiano, if desired.

Kosher salt

1 pound fusilli

1½ pounds beefsteak tomatoes (about 4 large tomatoes)

¼ cup olive oil

2 garlic cloves, smashed and peeled

3 fresh basil sprigs

½ cup whole-milk ricotta, plus more (optional) for serving

1¼ cups freshly grated Parmigiano-Reggiano, plus more (optional) for serving

¼ cup fresh basil leaves, chopped

lemon and pea alfredo

YIELD:
SERVES 6

SERVE WITH:
**TOMATO, AVOCADO, AND
ESCAROLE SALAD**

Fusilli con buco is one of my favorite pasta shapes for a creamy sauce like Alfredo that coats the long curlicues, and they're fun to eat because they can be scooped up with a fork without any twirling. This is a summery take on Alfredo, with the bright colors (and flavors) of lemon and peas and mascarpone.

Kosher salt

**1 pound fusilli con buco
(see Cook's Note)
or other long pasta**

3 tablespoons unsalted butter

1 garlic clove, minced

**2½ cups freshly grated
Parmigiano-Reggiano, plus
more (optional) for serving**

**1 cup mascarpone cheese,
at room temperature**

**2 teaspoons grated
lemon zest**

1½ cups frozen peas, thawed

**1 tablespoon freshly squeezed
lemon juice**

**1 teaspoon pink peppercorns,
ground**

COOK'S NOTE: Look for pasta brands such as Rustichella d'Abruzzo or Setaro.

Bring a large pot of salted water to a boil over high heat. Add the pasta and cook until just under al dente, 10 to 11 minutes.

Meanwhile, once you've added the pasta to the boiling water, heat a large straight-sided skillet over medium heat. Add the butter to the hot pan. When the butter is melted, add the garlic and cook, stirring often, until soft and fragrant, about 1 minute. Add ½ cup of water from the pasta pot and reduce the heat to low.

When the pasta is ready, transfer it to the pan with the sauce using tongs; reserve the pot of cooking water. Raise the heat to medium and sprinkle 1½ cups of the Parmigiano-Reggiano onto the plain pasta. Stir with 2 wooden spoons to combine. Add the mascarpone, lemon zest, and ¾ teaspoon salt. Toss well to coat, adding additional hot pasta water as needed to thin the sauce and to finish cooking the pasta. Add the peas, lemon juice, and the remaining 1 cup of Parmigiano-Reggiano. Toss well to combine, adding pasta water as needed to thin the sauce to your desired consistency; you will probably use close to 1½ cups pasta water total. Sprinkle with the ground pink peppercorns and additional Parmigiano-Reggiano, if desired.

sweet onion carbonara

Here again, I've updated a beloved pasta standard, adding a note of sweetness with lots of tender melted onions. This is a perfect decadent weeknight meal or brunch pasta. With all those yummy onions and cheese, it's pretty hard to mess this up; just don't scramble the eggs.

YIELD:
SERVES 6

SERVE WITH:
WILTED BABY KALE

Heat the olive oil in a large heavy skillet over medium heat. Add the pancetta and sauté until it is brown and crisp, about 8 minutes. Remove the pancetta from the pan and cool. Add the onions to the pan and cook for 10 minutes, or until golden brown and lightly caramelized. Add the garlic and ½ teaspoon salt, and cook 2 minutes more. Set aside to cool slightly. In a large bowl, combine the cream, ¼ teaspoon salt, the Parmigiano-Reggiano, Gruyère, lemon zest, and eggs, and whisk to blend.

Meanwhile, bring a large pot of salted water to a boil over high heat. Add the pasta and cook, stirring occasionally, until it is just tender but still firm to the bite, 8 to 10 minutes. Drain well, reserving 1 cup of the pasta cooking water.

Return the pasta to the large pot along with the onions, egg-and-cream mixture, ¼ cup of the reserved pasta water, and the pancetta. Toss over low heat until the sauce coats the pasta thickly, about 2 minutes, adding more pasta water as needed. Don't let the mixture get too hot or the eggs will scramble. Season to taste with pepper.

Transfer the pasta to a large wide serving bowl. Sprinkle with chives and serve.

2 teaspoons olive oil

4 ounces thinly sliced pancetta, chopped

1 large or 2 small yellow onions, halved and thinly sliced

2 garlic cloves, minced

Kosher salt

⅔ cup heavy cream

½ cup freshly grated Parmigiano-Reggiano

¾ cup shredded Gruyère cheese

½ teaspoon grated lemon zest

4 large eggs

1 pound mezzi rigatoni

Lots of coarsely ground black pepper

2 tablespoons chopped fresh chives

penne with corn and spicy sausage

YIELD:
SERVES 4 TO 6

SERVE WITH:
SIMPLE ARUGULA SALAD

Orecchiette with sausage is a staple in every Italian home, and this is my spin on it. Jade requests this dish weekly, and it literally takes fifteen minutes to make. The best part is it makes great leftovers that she can take to school the next day, and I love that!

Kosher salt

1 pound penne rigate

2 tablespoons extra-virgin olive oil

¾ pound spicy Italian sausage (about 4 links), casings removed

2 shallots, diced

2 cups frozen corn, thawed

8 ounces mascarpone cheese, at room temperature

1 tablespoon Calabrian chile paste

1 cup freshly grated Parmigiano-Reggiano, plus more (optional) for serving

¼ cup loosely packed fresh basil leaves, chopped

Bring a large pot of salted water to a boil over medium-high heat. Add the penne and cook according to package directions until al dente. Drain well, reserving ½ cup of the pasta cooking water.

Meanwhile, heat a medium skillet over medium-high heat. Add the olive oil and sausage, and cook for about 5 minutes, breaking up the sausage with a wooden spoon to form bite-size pieces. Add the shallots and cook for another minute. Stir in the corn and ½ teaspoon salt, and cook an additional 2 minutes, stirring often, until the corn is warmed through. Transfer the mixture to a large bowl.

To the bowl, add the mascarpone, chile paste, hot pasta, and reserved pasta water. Before tossing, sprinkle the Parmigiano-Reggiano directly onto the hot pasta to coat it with the cheese; this will help the sauce cling to the pasta better. Using a large serving spoon, mix together the corn mixture and Parmigiano-Reggiano–coated pasta. Add the basil and toss again. Serve with additional Parmigiano-Reggiano, if desired.

orzo with clams

Clam sauce is usually served with a long pasta, like linguine, but I've always thought orzo works much better. When you combine it with the seafood, the rice-shaped pasta collects in the shells, so I can eat it with a spoon and get a bit of both in every bite. The fennel and orange create a light, fresh broth. It's an unexpectedly elegant weeknight meal that doesn't take much effort.

YIELD:
SERVES 4

SERVE WITH:
GRILLED TREVISO WITH CITRUS BAGNA CAUDA

Heat a large straight-sided skillet over medium heat. Add the olive oil and heat 30 seconds more. Add the fennel, shallot, and salt to the hot pan. Cook, stirring often with a wooden spoon, until the fennel has softened, about 4 minutes. Add the peppers and chile paste, and cook another minute. Add the orzo and stir to coat the pasta in the oil. Add 2¼ cups water to the pan and stir to combine. Bring the mixture to a simmer and continue to cook for about 6 minutes, or 3 minutes less than the pasta package instructions. Add the clams to the skillet and cover with a lid. Cook an additional 3 to 4 minutes, occasionally shaking the pan, until the clams have opened. Discard any unopened clams. Stir the clams into the orzo and sprinkle with the fennel fronds and orange zest. Serve immediately.

3 tablespoons olive oil

1 small fennel bulb, trimmed and chopped

1 shallot, chopped

½ teaspoon kosher salt

5 jarred piquillo peppers, diced

½ teaspoon Calabrian chile paste

1 cup orzo

1 pound Manila clams or small littlenecks, scrubbed and rinsed

2 tablespoons fennel fronds, roughly chopped

1 teaspoon grated orange zest

mezzi rigatoni with butternut squash and spicy sausage

YIELD:
SERVES 4 TO 6

SERVE WITH:
CHARRED BROCCOLI RABE

I've learned that whenever I add sausage to pasta or veggies, Jade will eat them, so I do it often, and as a result I have greatly expanded the variety of vegetables in rotation at our house. Cooking the squash in the fat rendered from the sausage really deepens its flavor in a way that meat lovers will appreciate. Try it if you love squash, and if not, I still think this might change your mind about butternut squash.

Kosher salt

1 pound mezzi rigatoni

5 tablespoons extra-virgin olive oil

1 pound spicy Italian sausage, casings removed

1 pound butternut squash, peeled and cut in ⅓-inch pieces

1 cup freshly grated Parmigiano-Reggiano

2 cups roughly chopped baby arugula

Bring a large pot of salted water to a boil over high heat. Add the pasta and cook for 8 to 10 minutes, or just until al dente. Drain well, reserving ½ cup of the pasta cooking water, and set aside.

In a large skillet, heat 2 tablespoons of the olive oil over medium-high heat. Add the sausage and cook, breaking it up into bite-size pieces with a wooden spoon, until the sausage is cooked through, about 5 minutes. Add the diced squash to the skillet and stir to combine. Add 1½ cups water and season with ¼ teaspoon salt. Make sure all of the squash is submerged, pushing it down with the wooden spoon. Reduce the heat to medium and simmer until the squash is tender and the liquid has reduced by half, about 10 minutes.

Add the cooked pasta and ¾ cup of the Parmigiano-Reggiano to the skillet. Stir vigorously to combine, breaking up the squash a bit and thinning the mixture with the reserved pasta water as needed until the pasta is coated in a light and creamy sauce. Stir in the arugula and the remaining 3 tablespoons olive oil. Cook just until the arugula is wilted, about 2 minutes. Top with the remaining ¼ cup Parmigiano-Reggiano and serve.

bitter rice

The title of this dish is an homage to my grandmother Silvana Mangano's first film, *Bitter Rice*. The radicchio does have a wonderful, slightly bitter edge that is offset by the sweet cranberries. My grandmother (aka Nonna Luna) was a lover of rice dishes like this one, which is rich and flavorful enough to serve as an entrée for four, though it also works well as a side for six to eight people. If you are serving it with a roast, add some broth to loosen it a bit.

YIELD:
SERVES 4

SERVE WITH:
**ZUCCHINI SOTTOLIO
PANE POMODORO**

Place a medium Dutch oven over medium heat. Add the olive oil, chopped shallot, garlic, and ½ teaspoon of the salt to the pot. Stir with a wooden spoon. Cook until the shallots are soft and fragrant, about 4 minutes.

Add the rice and saffron to the pot and stir to coat the rice in the flavorful oil. Toast the rice for 2 minutes, stirring often. Add the wine and cook, stirring constantly, until almost all the liquid is absorbed. When the wine is absorbed, reduce the heat to medium-low and begin adding the broth ¾ cup at a time, stirring often between additions to release the starches and waiting until the broth has been almost entirely absorbed before adding more. This will take about 20 minutes.

When the last addition of broth is almost absorbed but there is still a thick liquid surrounding the rice, stir in the remaining ¼ teaspoon salt, the butter, Parmigiano-Reggiano, radicchio, cranberries, and black pepper. Stir until the radicchio is wilted and the cheese and butter are melted. The mixture should not be too stiff; add a bit more broth if needed to loosen the consistency. Serve with additional grated Parmigiano-Reggiano, if desired.

3 tablespoons olive oil

1 large shallot, chopped

1 garlic clove, chopped

¾ teaspoon kosher salt

1 cup Arborio rice

¼ teaspoon saffron threads

1 cup dry white wine

2¼ cups low-sodium chicken broth

¼ cup (½ stick) unsalted butter

1½ cups freshly grated Parmigiano-Reggiano, plus more (optional) for serving

1 small head radicchio, chopped into 1-inch pieces

⅓ cup dried cranberries

⅛ teaspoon freshly ground black pepper

italian chicken and rice

YIELD:
SERVES 4

SERVE WITH:
TOMATO, AVOCADO, AND ESCAROLE SALAD

This recipe also came from my grandmother (that's her with me, opposite!), but she never really wrote down the measurements. You need just one pot (a mom's dream!), and it's very comforting. My aunt Raffy has been making it for years, but sometimes hers came out too dry, so a couple of years ago, she asked me to take a crack at the recipe. I couldn't resist jazzing it up a bit with fresh herbs and a Parmigiano-Reggiano rind. Leftovers travel well, so this is great to pop in a lunch box. It's now a staple weeknight dish at my house.

2 tablespoons (¼ stick) unsalted butter

1 pound chicken tenders

1 teaspoon kosher salt

1 large red onion, diced

2 garlic cloves, smashed and peeled

1 cup basmati rice

½ teaspoon Calabrian chile paste

1 cup whole milk

½ cup low-sodium chicken broth

2 fresh sage sprigs

3 fresh thyme sprigs

1 (2-inch) piece of Parmigiano-Reggiano rind

¾ cup frozen peas

Freshly grated Parmigiano-Reggiano, for serving

Extra-virgin olive oil, to finish

Heat a medium straight-sided skillet over medium-high heat. Melt the butter in the skillet, leaving it until the bubbles subside. Season the chicken tenders evenly on both sides with ½ teaspoon of the salt. Add the chicken tenders to the pan in one layer. Cook the chicken for about 4 minutes per side, or until golden brown. (They don't need to be cooked through at this stage; they will cook further with the rice.) Transfer the chicken to a plate and set it aside.

Reduce the heat to medium. Add the onion and garlic to the pan, along with the remaining ½ teaspoon salt. Cook, stirring often, until the onions are softened and beginning to caramelize, about 4 minutes. Add the rice and chile paste, and cook, stirring frequently, for an additional 2 minutes to toast the rice. Add the milk, chicken broth, sage, thyme, and cheese rind, and stir to combine.

Return the chicken tenders and their juices to the pan, nestling the chicken down into the rice. Cover the pan and reduce the heat to low. Simmer for 15 minutes. Turn off the heat and sprinkle the peas on top. Replace the cover and allow the mixture to steam for an additional 12 minutes off the heat. Remove the herbs and rind from the pan and discard. Fluff the rice with a fork. Serve with grated Parmigiano-Reggiano and a drizzle of extra-virgin olive oil.

crispy chicken thighs with peppers and capers

YIELD:
SERVES 4

SERVE WITH:
**WHITE BEANS AND
TUSCAN KALE**

The inspiration for this dish comes from my great-aunt Raffy (Aunt Raffy's namesake), who makes the most delicious *peperonata*, a combination of sautéed peppers, olives, and capers that melts in your mouth. It makes the perfect bed for crispy chicken thighs. To get the skin perfectly crackly and delicious, sear the thighs in a *very hot* pan for a full 8 minutes—dark golden brown is what you're looking for.

¼ cup olive oil

**4 chicken thighs
(about 2 pounds)**

1 teaspoon kosher salt

**1 anchovy fillet or ½ teaspoon
anchovy paste**

**1 red bell pepper, cored,
seeded, and sliced into
thin strips**

1 shallot, diced small

**½ cup pitted kalamata olives,
roughly chopped**

**2 tablespoons capers,
drained and rinsed**

¼ teaspoon dried oregano

1 cup dry bread crumbs

**1 tablespoon flat-leaf parsley
leaves, chopped**

Preheat the oven to 425°F.

Heat 2 tablespoons of the olive oil in a medium skillet over medium-high heat. Dry the chicken very well with paper towels and season evenly on both sides with ¾ teaspoon of the salt. Place the thighs in the hot pan, skin-side down, and cook without moving for about 8 minutes, or until dark golden brown. Flip the thighs and cook an additional 3 minutes. Transfer the thighs to a baking sheet and roast for 10 to 15 minutes, or until an instant-read thermometer registers 160°F.

While the chicken roasts, place the same pan over medium heat and add the remaining 2 tablespoons olive oil. Add the anchovy and mash it with the back of a wooden spoon until it dissolves into the oil. Add the bell pepper and remaining ¼ teaspoon salt to the pan and cook, stirring often, for 5 minutes, until cooked through and soft. Stir in the shallots and cook an additional minute. Add the olives, capers, and oregano to the pan and stir to combine.

Sprinkle the bread crumbs over the pepper mixture and stir with a wooden spoon until the bread crumbs have soaked up all the flavored oil. Cook, stirring constantly, until the bread crumbs are toasted and the flavors have married, about another 3 minutes. Stir in the parsley. Spoon the bread-crumb mixture onto a platter. Top with the chicken thighs and drizzle with any accumulated juices from the baking sheet.

italian sheet-pan chicken with bread salad

How do you revamp a classic? Turn all the flavors of a cacciatore into a great tasty marinade, and then roast the marinated chicken on a sheet pan to speed up the cooking time. Marinate the chicken in the morning, and since it only needs 30 minutes in the oven, this is totally doable for a weeknight. I've boosted the seasonings with smoked paprika, which isn't traditional but really amps up the flavor. It's even better served over bread salad (as they do at San Francisco's famed Zuni Café).

YIELD:
SERVES 4

SERVE WITH:
WHITE CHOCOLATE ORZO PUDDING

FOR THE CHICKEN

1 garlic clove, smashed and peeled

½ teaspoon onion powder

1 teaspoon fennel seeds, toasted (see Cook's Notes)

1 teaspoon dried oregano

¾ teaspoon kosher salt

½ teaspoon smoked hot paprika

3 tablespoons vegetable juice cocktail, such as V8

3 tablespoons extra-virgin olive oil

1 (3-pound) chicken, cut in 6 pieces (see Cook's Notes)

FOR THE BREAD SALAD

3 cups diced rustic Italian bread

2 tablespoons olive oil

1½ cups freshly grated Parmigiano-Reggiano

1 cup cherry tomatoes, halved

1 small fennel bulb, stalks removed, thinly sliced

½ cup loosely packed fresh basil leaves, torn

1 tablespoon fresh lemon juice

Extra-virgin olive oil, as needed

MARINATE THE CHICKEN: Place the garlic, onion powder, fennel seeds, oregano, salt, paprika, vegetable juice, and olive oil in the bowl of a food processor. Puree until it forms a rough paste. Place the chicken pieces in a resealable plastic bag. Add the paste to the bag and rub the marinade all over the chicken pieces. Seal the bag and marinate in the refrigerator for at least 4 hours and up to 8 hours.

Place one rack in the middle of the oven and another in the top third of the oven. Preheat the oven to 400°F.

recipe continues »

Remove the chicken from the bag and arrange the pieces on a rimmed baking sheet. Place in the oven on the middle rack and roast for 30 minutes.

MEANWHILE, PREPARE THE BREAD SALAD: In a large bowl, toss the diced bread cubes with the olive oil and ½ cup of the Parmigiano-Reggiano. When the chicken has roasted for 30 minutes, remove the baking sheet from the oven and scatter the bread cubes around the chicken pieces. Return to the oven, this time on the top rack, and cook 15 to 20 minutes longer, or until the bread is toasted and the chicken is golden brown and registers 160°F on an instant-read thermometer. Remove from the oven and let the chicken rest for 10 minutes.

In the same large bowl used for the bread cubes, combine the tomatoes, fennel, basil, lemon juice, the toasted bread cubes, the remaining Parmigiano-Reggiano, and all of the juices from the chicken tray. Add a bit of extra-virgin olive oil, if needed, depending on the amount of juice from the chicken, and toss well. Serve the bread salad alongside the roasted chicken.

COOK'S NOTES: To toast the fennel seeds, place the seeds in a small dry skillet over medium heat. Toast them, stirring often, for 2 to 3 minutes, or until fragrant.

Ask your butcher to cut the chicken into leg, thigh, and breast/wing portions, or substitute an equal weight of chicken parts.

chicken agrodolce

I'm always looking for new ways to jazz up boneless chicken breasts, because both kids and adults eat them and they are so convenient, but the meat can be dry and bland if not seasoned correctly. This sweet and tangy sauce, which is served with everything from pork to vegetables in the northern part of Italy, keeps the meat moist. The best part is you don't need to marinate the chicken.

YIELD:
SERVES 4

SERVE WITH:
WILTED BABY KALE
PARMESAN ROASTED POTATOES

Preheat the oven to 375°F.

Heat a large ovenproof skillet over medium-high heat. Season the chicken evenly with the salt. Add the olive oil to the hot pan and heat 30 seconds. Add the chicken and cook without moving it for 5 to 6 minutes. Flip the breasts and sear on the other side for 3 minutes. Reduce the heat to medium and add the vinegar, garlic, thyme, and honey to the pan. Swirl to combine. Using tongs, flip each piece of chicken to coat it in the sauce. Place the pan in the oven and cook the chicken for approximately 15 minutes, or until an instant-read thermometer inserted in the thickest part of the breast registers 160°F. Baste with the sauce halfway through cooking.

Remove the pan from the oven and transfer the chicken to a platter to rest. Place the pan back over medium heat and simmer the pan juices for about 3 minutes, or until slightly thickened. Add the butter and whisk until melted and incorporated. Drizzle the chicken with the sauce and serve.

4 skinless, boneless chicken breasts (about 8 ounces each)

1 teaspoon kosher salt

2 tablespoons olive oil

½ cup balsamic vinegar

2 garlic cloves, smashed and peeled

4 fresh thyme sprigs

3 tablespoons mild-flavored honey, such as acacia or clover

2 tablespoons (¼ stick) unsalted butter

spicy turkey polpetone

YIELD:
SERVES 8 TO 10

SERVE WITH:
CREAMY POLENTA WITH SPINACH

For many people, meatballs are synonymous with Italian home cooking, but in our home, meat loaf (known as *polpetone*) was a much more typical meal. It's homey and kid-friendly, but because you don't need to shape and form individual meatballs, it comes together much more quickly. What gives this meat loaf its juicy flavor is the Italian sausage. Smoked hot paprika gives it a nice warmth and richness, similar to what you would get in traditional meat loaf.

2 (1-inch) slices of ciabatta or country white bread, crusts removed, diced (about 1 cup)

½ cup whole milk

1 large egg

½ cup freshly grated pecorino cheese

½ cup freshly grated Parmigiano-Reggiano

½ teaspoon dried oregano

½ teaspoon smoked hot paprika

Pinch of crushed red pepper flakes (optional)

¾ teaspoon kosher salt

½ pound spicy Italian turkey sausage, casings removed

1 pound ground white meat turkey

1 tablespoon olive oil

1 (24-ounce) jar of store-bought marinara sauce

Preheat the oven to 375°F.

In a medium bowl, mix together the diced ciabatta, milk, and egg, breaking up the bread with your fingers. Let the mixture soak for 10 minutes.

To the bread mixture, add the cheeses, oregano, paprika, red pepper flakes (if using), salt, sausage, and ground turkey. Using your hands, mix until evenly combined, making sure the sausage and turkey are well distributed.

Drizzle the olive oil on a rimmed baking sheet. Mound the meat mixture on the baking sheet and use your hands to pat it into a 1½-inch-thick loaf. Spread ½ cup of the marinara over the loaf.

Bake the polpetone for 45 minutes, or until an instant-read thermometer inserted in the thickest part registers 160°F. Allow the loaf to rest for 10 minutes before slicing. Warm the remaining marinara in a small saucepan and serve alongside.

a tale of two cheeses

Many, many Italian recipes call for a healthy addition of grated hard cheese, such as Parmigiano-Reggiano or Pecorino. Both of these cheeses add a savory, salty, umami boost to everything from pastas to salad dressings to meatballs. But I'm often asked if these two cheeses can be used interchangeably and why sometimes, as in this turkey meat loaf recipe, they are used in tandem. While you can, in many instances, swap out one of these cheeses for the other, they differ in both taste and texture. Parmigiano is made from cow's milk, and the best ones are aged, so the flavor is milder, with a nutty, buttery taste. It also has a drier, almost granular texture. Pecorino is a younger, tangier cheese made from sheep's milk and has more bite. Because it's not aged the way Parm is, it has more moisture. I like to combine the two because you get the perfect balance of salty-nuttiness, but if you are only going to use one, opt for Parm; an all-Pecorino dish would be too salty and tangy.

herb-roasted pork tenderloin

YIELD:
SERVES 4 TO 6

SERVE WITH:
**CHEESY MASHED POTATOES
STEAMED BROCCOLI**

Pork tenderloins are a godsend for weeknights because they marinate very quickly and cook even faster. Italians would serve this with a sprinkle of gremolata, but I love to moisten the pork with a whole-grain mustard dressing, which I drizzle on my salad, too. I've given both options, so have it your way!

FOR THE PORK

2 (1-pound) pork tenderloins, silver skin removed (see Cook's Note)

1 tablespoon chopped fresh rosemary leaves

3 garlic cloves, peeled and roughly chopped

1 teaspoon fennel seeds, lightly toasted (see Cook's Notes, page 134)

1 teaspoon kosher salt

2 tablespoons olive oil

FOR THE GREMOLATA

1 cup packed flat-leaf parsley leaves, chopped

1 teaspoon grated lemon zest

1 tablespoon fresh lemon juice

½ teaspoon kosher salt

¼ teaspoon freshly ground black pepper

½ cup extra-virgin olive oil

FOR THE DRESSING

2 tablespoons whole-grain mustard

¼ cup freshly grated Parmigiano-Reggiano

1 tablespoon champagne vinegar

3 tablespoons extra-virgin olive oil

¼ teaspoon kosher salt

Remove the pork from the fridge 15 minutes before you are ready to cook. Preheat the oven to 425°F.

Place the rosemary, garlic, and fennel seeds in a small pile on a cutting board. Run your knife through the pile a few times to chop everything finely and mix the ingredients together. Place the herb mix in a small bowl and add the salt and olive oil to make a paste. Using your hands, rub the paste all over the tenderloins.

Heat a large ovenproof skillet over medium-high heat. Sear the tenderloins in the pan for about 3 minutes per side, or until golden on all sides. Place the pan in the preheated oven and roast for approximately 8 minutes, or until an instant-read thermometer registers 145°F. Remove the pork from the oven and allow it to rest for 10 minutes before slicing.

While the pork rests, make your desired topping. If using the gremolata, whisk together the parsley, lemon zest, lemon juice, salt, pepper, and olive oil. Set aside.

If serving with the mustard dressing, combine the mustard, Parmigiano-Reggiano, vinegar, olive oil, and salt in a jar with a tight-fitting lid. Shake vigorously to emulsify. Set aside to let the flavors marry for 5 minutes or so.

Serve the sliced pork with either a sprinkle of gremolata or a drizzle of the dressing.

COOK'S NOTE: Silver skin is a thin, sinewy membrane that encases the tenderloin. If it has not already been removed, use a sharp knife to trim it off, removing as little of the meat as possible.

flank steak with roasted grapes and mushrooms

Mushrooms and grapes both grow all over northern Italy, and I used this classic pairing to make a topping for crostini, then took some of the mixture to dress up a flank steak for a dinner party. Everyone loved it, and it's a nice change from bottled steak sauce with some of the same sweet/savory notes.

YIELD:
SERVES 4 TO 6

SERVE WITH:
**POTATO CRISPS WITH GOAT CHEESE AND OLIVES
TOMATO, AVOCADO, AND ESCAROLE SALAD**

Preheat the oven to 400°F.

Heat 1 tablespoon of the olive oil in a large skillet over high heat. Season the steak evenly on both sides with 1½ teaspoons of the salt. Place the steak in the skillet and cook without moving it for 5 minutes, or until deep golden brown. Using tongs, flip the steak and sear the other side for an additional 3 minutes.

Transfer the steak to a rimmed baking sheet and roast for 10 to 12 minutes, or until an instant-read thermometer inserted in the thickest part registers 125°F. Remove the steak to a cutting board to rest for at least 10 minutes.

While the steak is in the oven, place the skillet over medium-high heat and add the remaining 2 tablespoons olive oil. Add the mushrooms to the skillet and season with ¼ teaspoon of the salt. Cook, stirring occasionally with a wooden spoon, for about 8 minutes, or until the mushrooms are deep golden brown all over. Add the shallots and the remaining ¼ teaspoon salt, and cook 2 minutes longer, stirring often. Stir in the sherry, scraping up any bits from the bottom of the pan, and cook until it has reduced by half, 2 to 3 minutes. Add the grapes, beef stock, and thyme, and cook an additional 2 minutes. Add the butter and swirl the pan while stirring with the wooden spoon to emulsify the sauce. Remove from the heat.

Slice the steak against the grain about ⅓ inch thick. Fan the slices on a platter and spoon the mushrooms over the steak.

3 tablespoons olive oil

1 (1½- to 1¾-pound) flank steak

2 teaspoons kosher salt

¾ pound assorted wild mushrooms, such as royal trumpets and cremini, sliced ¼ inch thick

2 shallots, finely chopped

½ cup dry sherry

1 cup halved seedless red grapes

½ cup beef stock

½ teaspoon fresh thyme leaves, chopped

2 tablespoons (¼ stick) unsalted butter

pan-seared branzino with tomato and capers

YIELD:
SERVES 2 TO 4

SERVE WITH:
ORZO
SHAVED ARTICHOKE
AND FENNEL SALAD
CIABATTA

This is the fastest fish dish you will ever make and my first choice when I have friends coming over for a quick weeknight get-together. It's super colorful and impressive, with the flavors of Positano in every bite. This will serve four if you have a first course or are eating lighter; otherwise, serve two fillets per person.

4 skin-on branzino fillets

½ teaspoon kosher salt

2 tablespoons extra-virgin olive oil

1 cup cherry tomatoes, quartered

2 tablespoons capers, drained and rinsed

½ cup pitted niçoise olives, halved

3 tablespoons dry white wine

1 tablespoon unsalted butter

2 tablespoons chopped fresh flat-leaf parsley

Heat a large skillet over medium-high heat. Pat the branzino fillets very dry with paper towels and check to make sure there are no small bones remaining in the flesh. Score the skin side of the fish with a sharp knife by making 3 shallow cuts on a slight diagonal on each fillet. Season the fillets evenly on all sides with the salt.

Pour the olive oil in the hot pan. Place the fillets in the pan, skin-side down. Press gently on each fillet to make sure the skin has full contact with the hot pan. Allow the fish to cook undisturbed for 3 minutes. Using a fish spatula, gently flip each fillet and cook for another 30 seconds on the flesh side. Remove the branzino to a platter, skin-side up, and keep warm.

To the hot pan, add the tomatoes, capers, and olives. Cook for 1 minute, stirring often with a wooden spoon. Add the white wine, reduce the heat to medium, and cook for an additional 2 minutes to reduce the wine by half. Add the butter and parsley, swirling the pan to incorporate the butter as it melts. Spoon the sauce over the branzino and serve.

grilled swordfish with candied lemon salad

YIELD:
SERVES 4

SERVE WITH:
ZUCCHINI SOTTOLIO ON GRILLED PEASANT BREAD

I've been making and eating a salad with candied lemon pieces for years, because I love all things lemony. I guess I'm not alone, because it was a hit when I put it on my Vegas menu. It's a wonderful complement to a dense fish like swordfish; the candied lemons brighten and lighten up the fish perfectly, and adding some protein makes the salad feel more like a meal.

FOR THE CANDIED LEMON SALAD

2 lemons

¼ cup sugar

1 teaspoon Dijon mustard

2 tablespoons extra-virgin olive oil

1 tablespoon chopped fresh basil

⅛ teaspoon plus ¼ teaspoon kosher salt

¾ cup Castelvetrano olives, pitted and halved

4 cups baby arugula

FOR THE SWORDFISH

4 (6-ounce) skinless swordfish or tuna steaks (see Cook's Notes)

1 teaspoon kosher salt

2 tablespoons olive oil

With a sharp knife, cut the ends off the lemons. Standing one upright on one end, slice off the rind, following the curve of the fruit and removing all the white pith. Holding the lemon in your hand, cut between the membranes to free the segments, collecting them in a small bowl. Repeat with the remaining lemon.

In a small saucepan, combine the sugar with 2 tablespoons water. Set over medium heat and bring to a simmer, stirring occasionally, to dissolve the sugar, a minute or two. Add the lemon segments and simmer for another 2 minutes. Remove from the heat and allow the lemons to cool in the liquid.

Using a slotted spoon, transfer the segments to a small bowl and reserve the sugar syrup. In a medium bowl, whisk together the mustard and 2 tablespoons of the sugar syrup (see Cook's Notes). Whisk in the olive oil, basil, and ⅛ teaspoon salt. Set aside half of the dressing for the fish. To the remaining dressing, add the olives, arugula, and reserved lemon segments but do not toss everything together. Set aside.

Preheat a grill pan over medium-high heat. Dry the fish well using paper towels and season with the 1 teaspoon salt and the olive oil. Grill the fish for 3 to 4 minutes per side, depending on the thickness of the steaks; they should be golden brown and release easily from the pan before you turn them. Toss the salad with the dressing in the bottom of the bowl, adding the remaining ¼ teaspoon salt. Place a piece of fish on each plate and top with some of the salad. Spoon the remaining dressing around the fish.

COOK'S NOTES: In Italy, this would be made with swordfish, which is quite plentiful, but you can certainly substitute tuna.

Save any remaining lemon syrup for another use; it will keep for weeks in a covered container in the refrigerator. In the summer I use it to flavor cocktails and iced tea.

salmon with puttanesca

The bold flavors of anchovies, capers, and olives are the backbone of puttanesca, a southern Italian red sauce made with ingredients common to the region. It's more often served over pasta, but like so many Italian sauces, this one can be served with just about anything that needs a gutsy accent. I find many people, including me, are eating more fish and chicken these days; if you're looking for a way to change it up, this will become a weeknight staple.

YIELD:
SERVES 4

SERVE WITH:
**SAUTÉED SPINACH
ROASTED PARMIGIANO-
REGGIANO POTATOES**

FOR THE SAUCE

**4 jarred piquillo peppers
or 1 roasted red bell pepper**

1 tablespoon tomato paste

½ teaspoon anchovy paste

**2 tablespoons capers,
drained and rinsed**

**⅓ cup pitted kalamata olives,
rinsed**

1 garlic clove

⅛ teaspoon kosher salt

¼ cup extra-virgin olive oil

FOR THE SALMON

**4 (6-ounce) skinless
center-cut wild salmon fillets**

1 teaspoon kosher salt

2 tablespoons olive oil

In the bowl of a food processor, combine the peppers, tomato paste, anchovy paste, capers, olives, garlic, and salt. Puree until smooth, scraping down the sides of the machine with a rubber spatula as needed. With the machine running, add 1 tablespoon of water, then add the extra-virgin olive oil in a steady stream until the mixture is emulsified and smooth. Set aside.

Dry the salmon fillets well with paper towels. Season evenly with the salt. Heat a large nonstick skillet over medium-high heat. Add the olive oil and heat for 30 seconds longer. Lay the salmon fillets in the pan, flesh-side down. Cook the fish without moving it for 3 to 4 minutes, or until the fillets are golden and are becoming brown and opaque at the edges. Flip the fish and cook for an additional 3 to 4 minutes.

Spread some of the sauce on the bottom of each plate and place a piece of salmon on top. Drizzle with a little extra sauce, if desired.

flounder piccata

Piccata is a classic Italian preparation that most often uses veal or chicken scaloppini, but like many Italian sauces, it can be used with lots of different proteins. I especially like the way it brightens up the flavor of seafood. Flounder is a mild-flavored fish similar to cod, which you can substitute for the flounder, and both are quick to cook and good "unfishy" fish for kids. The sauce is quick, too, and nicely tangy and lemony. I sometimes top it with toasted bread crumbs for an extra crunch! You can have this on the table in about 20 minutes, I promise.

YIELD:
SERVES 4

SERVE WITH:
BITTER RICE
STEAMED BROCCOLI

In a shallow bowl, combine ½ teaspoon of the salt with the flour. Set aside.

Heat a large skillet over medium-high heat. Add 1 tablespoon each of the butter and olive oil to the hot pan and heat until the butter is melted and the foam has subsided. Dredge a piece of flounder in the flour, making sure to coat both sides. Add the fish to the hot pan and repeat with one more fillet. Cook for 4 minutes on the first side, or until deep golden brown and almost completely cooked through. Gently flip the fish and cook an additional 1 to 2 minutes, or just until cooked through. Remove the fish to a platter. Add another tablespoon of butter and olive oil to the pan and repeat with the remaining fish fillets. Tent the platter with foil to keep the fish warm.

To the hot pan, add the lemon slices and capers. Cook, stirring often with a wooden spoon, for about 2 minutes, or until the capers are beginning to open and the lemons are starting to brown. Add the chicken broth and simmer for about 3 minutes to reduce by a third. Stir in the remaining 2 tablespoons butter and season with the remaining ¼ teaspoon salt. Spoon the sauce over the fish. Sprinkle with the parsley and serve.

¾ teaspoon kosher salt

½ cup Wondra or all-purpose flour (see Cook's Note)

4 tablespoons (½ stick) unsalted butter

2 tablespoons olive oil

4 flounder fillets (4 to 6 ounces each)

½ large lemon, thinly sliced

¼ cup capers, drained and rinsed

½ cup low-sodium chicken broth

¼ cup fresh flat-leaf parsley leaves, chopped

COOK'S NOTE: Wondra, a quick-mixing flour that contains rye as well as wheat flour, makes for the crispiest crust. Another good choice is Cup4Cup or a similar gluten-free baking blend.

pan-seared salmon with artichokes and white wine

YIELD:
SERVES 4

SERVE WITH:
**ENDIVE, PANCETTA, AND
TOMATO SALAD**

The crust on this salmon is everything, so be patient and don't move the fillets until they get a good, hard sear. Aside from the fish, almost every element of this light, colorful dish is a pantry item, which makes it an easy weeknight meal. And you can never have too many ways to cook salmon.

2 tablespoons olive oil

4 (6-ounce) skinless center-cut salmon fillets

1 teaspoon kosher salt

2 tablespoons (¼ stick) unsalted butter

3 fresh oregano sprigs, plus 1 tablespoon chopped

1 shallot, sliced

1 (9-ounce) box frozen artichoke hearts, thawed

¾ cup chopped oil-packed sun-dried tomatoes

½ cup dry white wine

2 cups baby spinach

In a medium skillet, heat the olive oil over medium-high heat. Season the salmon fillets evenly with the salt and place them, flesh-side down (skin-side up), in the hot pan. Cook for 3 minutes, or until deep golden brown. Turn the fillets on their sides and cook for a minute, then turn to the opposite side and cook 1 minute longer. Lastly, using a thin spatula, flip the fillets and cook an additional 2 minutes. Add 1 tablespoon of butter and the oregano sprigs to the pan and reduce the heat to medium. Baste the salmon fillets with the infused butter for an additional minute. Remove the salmon and oregano sprigs to a plate to rest.

To the same pan, add the shallot and artichoke hearts. Cook over medium heat, stirring often with a wooden spoon, until the shallot is softened and the artichokes are beginning to brown, about 4 minutes. Add the chopped oregano and the tomatoes, and stir to combine. Deglaze the pan with the white wine and allow the wine to cook down and reduce by half. Stir in the remaining tablespoon of butter and the spinach. Cook until the spinach is just barely wilted. Spoon the vegetables onto a platter and top with the salmon. Spoon any remaining sauce over the fish and serve.

lemon sole oreganata

I borrowed this combination of flavors from the classic preparation for clams. It's light, easy, and fast. The Parmigiano-Reggiano bread-crumb mixture on top gives the fish a nice crunchy crust.

YIELD:
SERVES 4

SERVE WITH:
TOMATO, AVOCADO, AND ESCAROLE SALAD

¾ cup bread crumbs

1½ teaspoons dried oregano

1 teaspoon grated lemon zest

½ cup freshly grated Parmigiano-Reggiano

4 tablespoons olive oil

4 lemon sole fillets (about 8 ounces each)

1 teaspoon kosher salt

⅔ cup dry white wine

¼ cup fresh flat-leaf parsley leaves, roughly chopped

Lemon wedges, for serving

Position an oven rack in the top third of the oven. Preheat the oven to 450°F.

In a medium bowl, whisk together the bread crumbs, oregano, lemon zest, Parmigiano-Reggiano, and 3 tablespoons of the olive oil. The mixture should resemble wet sand. Set aside.

Brush the remaining 1 tablespoon olive oil over the bottom of a rimmed baking sheet. Place the sole fillets in a single layer on the sheet and season with the salt. Sprinkle the bread-crumb topping evenly over each fillet and pat gently to adhere. Pour the wine around the fish. Bake the fish for 10 minutes, or until barely cooked through.

Remove the sheet from the oven and heat the broiler to high.

Place the baking sheet under the broiler for an additional 1 to 2 minutes, or until the bread crumbs are nicely toasted and golden brown, and the fish is cooked through. Using a wide spatula, transfer the fillets to dinner plates, sprinkle with the parsley, and drizzle with any pan juices that remain. Serve with a lemon wedge to squeeze over the top.

monkfish cacciatore

YIELD:
SERVES 4

SERVE WITH:
**SPRING GREEN MIX SALAD
CREAMY POLENTA WITH
SPINACH**

Monkfish is a firm-textured and meaty fish with a sweet, light flavor that some say reminds them of lobster (maybe because their underwater diets are similar). Because cacciatore is a hearty sauce, it works really well with the firm fish (side note: any meaty, mild fish, such as halibut, will work). I'm trying to make weeknight dinners more varied and get Jade to try new things (like different fish) by topping them with sauces I know she likes.

**4 (6-ounce) monkfish fillets,
membranes removed
if needed**

1½ teaspoons kosher salt

¼ cup olive oil

**½ pound cremini mushrooms,
sliced**

1 red onion, chopped

**1 red bell pepper, cored,
seeded, and chopped**

**1 garlic clove, smashed
and peeled**

½ teaspoon dried oregano

**2 tablespoons capers,
drained and rinsed**

1 cup dry white wine

**1 (14-ounce) can baby Roma
or cherry tomatoes**

Dry the monkfish well and season it all over with 1 teaspoon of the salt. Heat 2 tablespoons of the olive oil in a medium nonreactive straight-sided skillet over medium-high heat until a whisper of smoke comes off the pan. Sear the fish in the pan until it is golden brown on all sides, about 8 minutes total. Remove the fish to a plate.

Add the mushrooms to the pan. Cook, stirring often with a wooden spoon and scraping up the bits from the bottom of the pan, until the mushrooms are a deep golden brown, about 6 minutes. Add the onion, bell pepper, garlic, and the remaining ½ teaspoon salt. Cook for 2 minutes to soften the vegetables slightly. Add the oregano and capers, and warm through, about 1 minute longer.

Add the wine and stir to loosen any bits from the bottom of the pan. Bring the wine to a simmer and cook gently for 3 minutes, or until reduced by half. Add the tomatoes and crush them gently with the back of a spoon. Stir in the remaining 2 tablespoons olive oil and return the mixture to a simmer. Reduce the heat to medium-low, nestle the fish in the sauce, and cover with a tight-fitting lid. Braise the fish for 8 to 10 minutes, turning the pieces halfway through to coat in the sauce. Serve each fillet with a generous spoonful of the sauce.

mussels in white wine

I ate this several times a week when I was shooting in Positano, and it's the kind of simple, satisfying meal you can get in any seaside café on the Amalfi coast. It's a little out of the box when it comes to weeknight cooking here at home, but it's so light and so flavorful you owe it to yourself to give it a try. Because the mussels make their own savory broth, you don't need to add much more than a bit of wine, butter, and fresh tarragon, so it's easy on the waistline, too!

YIELD:
SERVES 2

SERVE WITH:
SARDINIAN PASTA SALAD *OR* **TOMATO, AVOCADO, AND ESCAROLE SALAD**

Heat a medium Dutch oven over medium-high heat. Add the olive oil, shallot, and garlic, and cook for 3 minutes, stirring often, until the shallot is beginning to turn golden brown. Add the mussels and black pepper, and stir to coat them with the oil. Add the white wine and cover the pan with the lid. Steam the mussels for about 3 minutes, or until they have opened. Discard any unopened mussels.

Using a slotted spoon, scoop the mussels into a serving bowl. Add the butter to the juices in the pan and stir until the butter is melted and incorporated into the sauce. Pour the sauce over the mussels and sprinkle with the tarragon.

2 tablespoons olive oil

1 shallot, sliced

2 garlic cloves, smashed and peeled

2 pounds mussels, scrubbed and beards removed, if needed

½ teaspoon cracked black pepper

½ cup dry white wine

2 tablespoons (¼ stick) unsalted butter

2 tablespoons chopped fresh tarragon

SARTU DI RISO

SPICY LAMB BOLOGNESE

PENNE WITH
PARMIGIANO-REGGIANO
POMODORO

SPAGHETTI WITH
CHIANTI AND FAVA
BEANS

PENNE WITH PORK RAGU

ZITI STUFATI

CREAMY LOBSTER
LINGUINE

MUSHROOM AND
ASPARAGUS FARROTTO

BAROLO-BRAISED
SHORT RIBS

LAMB OSSO BUCO

ITALIAN SPRINGTIME
LAMB

MARINATED BISTECCA
FIORENTINA

TRICOLORE STUFFED
PORK

VEAL SALTIMBOCCA
MILANESE-STYLE

GRILLED CHICKEN
INVOLTINI

HAZELNUT CHICKEN

GRILLED SCALLOPS WITH
PROSCIUTTO AND BASIL

ITALIAN BARBECUED
SHRIMP

SLOW-ROASTED SALMON

WHOLE ROASTED FISH

la dolce vita

In Italy, like most places, everyone looks forward to the weekend—TGIF! That's when the big meals come out, and we all try to impress one another with food that's a little more special than what we might serve on a hurried weeknight. More than any others in the book, the recipes in this chapter really capture the essence of Italian life, those lazy, relaxed afternoons and evenings spent around the table with wine, food, and friends. They're meals that deserve to be lingered over. These dishes aren't necessarily all that difficult to prepare, but you will need to set aside a bit of time to make them. The upside is that when you cook up a big pot of short ribs or roast a leg of lamb, the whole house smells good; more important, when people know you've taken that extra minute to make their meal, they feel cared for and happy. Meals like these create memories. I hope they will help you cook up some delicious memories of your own.

sartu di riso

In Naples, its birthplace, this impressive dish is usually only made on Sunday, when the family is all together and can participate in the preparation. Like Ziti Stufati (page 173), it is served at weddings, first communions, and other important events. It's a dish I learned from my aunt Raffy and is honestly an investment of time, but it is a stunning centerpiece for a big celebration, and when it comes out of the mold you will feel very accomplished.

YIELD:
SERVES 8 TO 10

SERVE WITH:
**TORTELLINI IN PARMIGIANO-REGGIANO BRODO
ENDIVE, PANCETTA, AND TOMATO SALAD**

FOR THE RICE

1 pound Arborio rice (2⅓ cups)

4 cups low-sodium chicken broth

1 bay leaf

1¼ teaspoons kosher salt

2½ cups freshly grated Parmigiano-Reggiano

3 large eggs, at room temperature

FOR THE SAUCE

¼ cup olive oil

½ pound sweet Italian sausage or sweet Italian turkey sausage, casings removed

1 shallot, sliced

1 garlic clove, chopped

¼ teaspoon kosher salt

1 (28-ounce) can crushed tomatoes

2 fresh basil sprigs

1 (2-inch) piece of Parmigiano-Reggiano rind

FOR THE MEATBALL FILLING

2 tablespoons fine dry bread crumbs

3 tablespoons whole milk, at room temperature

1 large egg, at room temperature

½ teaspoon dried oregano

¼ teaspoon kosher salt

½ cup freshly grated Parmigiano-Reggiano

½ pound ground sirloin or ground dark meat turkey

Olive oil, for frying

1 cup frozen peas, thawed

8 ounces fresh mozzarella cheese (1 ball), diced

1½ tablespoons unsalted butter, at room temperature

5 tablespoons fine dry bread crumbs

MAKE THE RICE: In a large saucepan, combine the rice, chicken broth, bay leaf, and salt. Stir and bring to a boil over high heat. Cover the pan with a tight-fitting lid, reduce the heat to low, and simmer for 8 minutes, stirring once, until the rice is still slightly undercooked but the liquid is absorbed. Pour the rice into a large bowl and cool to room temperature, stirring occasionally. Stir in the Parmigiano-Reggiano and eggs until well combined and set aside.

recipe continues »

MAKE THE SAUCE: Heat the olive oil in a medium nonreactive saucepan over medium-high heat. Break the sausage into small bite-size pieces and add it to the hot oil. Cook, breaking it up with the back of a wooden spoon, until browned, about 5 minutes. Using a slotted spoon, remove the sausage to a medium bowl and set it aside. Reduce the heat under the pan to medium and add the shallot, garlic, and salt. Cook, stirring constantly for 1 minute, or until fragrant and the shallot is soft. Add the tomatoes, basil sprigs, and cheese rind, and bring to a simmer. Reduce the heat to low and simmer, stirring occasionally with a wooden spoon, for 15 to 20 minutes. Remove the basil and cheese rind, and discard. Add 2 cups of the sauce to the bowl with the sausage and reserve the rest.

MEANWHILE, MAKE THE MEATBALL FILLING: In a separate medium bowl, mix together the bread crumbs, milk, and egg with a fork and let the mixture sit for 5 minutes to thicken. Stir in the oregano, salt, and Parmigiano-Reggiano. Add the ground meat and mix, using your clean hands, until just combined. Scoop 1-tablespoon mounds of the mixture into your damp hands and roll it into uniform balls.

Heat ½ inch of olive oil in a medium straight-sided skillet. When the oil is hot, fry the balls in two batches, turning them as needed until golden brown and crisp all over; this will take about 4 minutes per batch. Using a slotted spoon, transfer the browned meatballs to the bowl with the sausage and sauce. Repeat with the remaining balls. Toss to coat the meatballs and sausage evenly with the sauce. Add the peas and diced mozzarella, and toss gently to incorporate.

Preheat the oven to 350°F.

TO ASSEMBLE, butter the inside of a Bundt pan or a 3½-quart Dutch oven, using 1 tablespoon of the butter to coat it very thoroughly. Dust the inside of the pan with 3 tablespoons of the bread crumbs. Make sure it is evenly coated and that there are no bald spots. (This is very important to prevent sticking.) Spoon two-thirds of the rice mixture into the prepared pan. Using damp hands, press the rice evenly over the bottom of the pan and 2½ inches up the sides and around the center tube. Spoon the meat filling into the well of rice and press gently to make sure it is evenly packed. Spoon the remaining rice mixture over the filling and, again using damp hands, press the rice mixture evenly over the filling, being sure to press the rice mixture on top into the rice along the edges to seal. Sprinkle evenly with the remaining 2 tablespoons bread crumbs and dot with the remaining ½ tablespoon butter.

Bake for 45 minutes, or until lightly browned on top. Remove from the oven and allow to rest in the pan for 15 minutes.

To serve, place a plate large enough to cover over the pan. Using pot holders or a towel, invert the *sartu* onto the plate. Carefully lift the pan off the rice, shaking gently, if needed, to loosen it. Warm the reserved sauce and ladle it into the center of the rice mold. Slice and serve immediately.

spicy lamb bolognese

Jade absolutely loves Bolognese sauce and has become quite a connoisseur, ordering it in restaurants wherever we go. This version is half lamb and half ground beef, a mixture you'll see a lot in northern Italy. Because the lamb is lean, this is a somewhat lighter sauce than all-beef or pork-based ragu. I've put the hearty, homey sauce in this section because it does need a good long simmer, but since it makes enough for two meals, you get a bonus quick-and-easy weeknight dinner for your investment of time. The pasta shouldn't be swimming in sauce; you only want it to stain the pasta. That's why it's important to use a good-quality pasta that has some tooth to it.

YIELD:
MAKES APPROXIMATELY 6 CUPS; SERVES 8 TO 12

SERVE WITH:
PARMIGIANO-REGGIANO AND PROSCIUTTO SPICED PRUNES MASCARPONE CANNOLI CHEESECAKE

2 tablespoons (¼ stick) unsalted butter

4 tablespoons olive oil, plus more for drizzling

1 onion, finely chopped

1 carrot, peeled and finely chopped

1 celery stalk, finely chopped

1 teaspoon kosher salt, plus more as needed

¾ pound ground lamb

¾ pound ground chuck (80% lean)

1 garlic clove, chopped

1 teaspoon Calabrian chile paste

½ teaspoon crushed red pepper flakes

¼ cup tomato paste

2 cups whole milk

1 cup dry red wine, such as Chianti

1 (28-ounce) can whole San Marzano tomatoes, crushed by hand

1 bay leaf

1 (3-inch) piece of Parmigiano-Reggiano rind

1 (8.8-ounce) package of pappardelle pasta

1 cup freshly grated Parmigiano-Reggiano

Heat a medium Dutch oven over medium heat. Add the butter and 2 tablespoons of the olive oil and heat until the butter is melted. Add the onion, carrot, celery, and ½ teaspoon of the salt. Cook, stirring often, for 6 minutes, or until the vegetables are soft but not yet beginning to brown. Add the lamb and beef, and cook, breaking apart the meat with a wooden spoon, for 5 minutes, or until the meat is cooked through and no longer pink. Stir in the garlic, chile paste, red pepper lakes, and tomato paste. Cook for 2 minutes, stirring often, to caramelize the tomato paste.

recipe continues »

Stir in the milk. Bring to a simmer and cook for 20 minutes, stirring occasionally, until the milk is almost entirely evaporated. Add the wine, tomatoes, bay leaf, cheese rind, and the remaining ½ teaspoon salt. Bring to a simmer, then reduce the heat to maintain a gentle simmer and cook the sauce for 2 hours, stirring occasionally to prevent sticking.

Skim the oil from the surface. Ladle half the sauce (about 3 cups) into a covered container and refrigerate for up to 4 days or freeze for up to 3 months for another meal. Transfer the remaining sauce to a large straight-sided skillet.

Bring a large pot of salted water to a boil over high heat. Add the pappardelle and cook 2 minutes less than the package directions, about 7 minutes.

Meanwhile, reheat the Bolognese gently over medium heat. Add ½ cup of the pasta cooking water to the sauce and bring to a simmer. Using tongs or a pasta fork, scoop the pappardelle directly into the pan with the sauce. Sprinkle the pasta with ¾ cup of the Parmigiano-Reggiano and, using 2 wooden spoons, toss the pasta with the sauce until well coated.

Continue to cook the pasta in the sauce, adding pasta water by ¼ cup as needed, until the pasta is cooked to al dente. Drizzle with the remaining 2 tablespoons olive oil and toss again to combine. Serve with the remaining Parmigiano-Reggiano and an additional drizzle of olive oil, if desired

penne with parmigiano-reggiano pomodoro

This is a weekend sauce because it uses all the cheese rinds an Italian cook would have accumulated over the course of the week. Canned cherry tomatoes make all the difference here; the sauce is so much sweeter and more delicate than if made with regular plum tomatoes! I make big batches for Jade's school auction every year.

YIELD:
SERVES 6

SERVE WITH:
HAM AND RICOTTA PINWHEELS
POUND CAKE WITH
LIMONCELLO ZABAGLIONE

Heat a medium nonreactive saucepan over medium-high heat. Add ⅓ cup of the olive oil and the garlic, and reduce the heat to medium. Cook the garlic for 5 minutes, stirring often and mashing gently with a wooden spoon, until golden brown and beginning to soften. Add the tomatoes and their juices, the basil, carrot, and cheese rinds. Stir with a wooden spoon to combine. Bring to a simmer and adjust the heat to maintain a simmer. Cook for 35 minutes, stirring occasionally to prevent sticking. Season the sauce with the 1 teaspoon salt. Remove from the heat and cool slightly.

Remove the rinds, carrot, and basil, and discard. At this point you can use an immersion blender to puree the sauce slightly or leave it chunky, as you prefer.

Bring a large pot of salted water to a boil over high heat. Add the penne and cook 2 minutes less than the package directions, about 12 minutes. Meanwhile, rewarm the sauce in a large straight-sided skillet over medium heat. Using a wire skimmer, scoop the pasta from the water (reserving the pasta cooking water) and add it directly to the pan with the sauce. Before stirring, sprinkle the pasta with the ½ cup grated Parmigiano-Reggiano. Toss the pasta, cheese, and sauce together. Add the butter, the remaining 2 tablespoons olive oil, and ½ cup of the pasta cooking water, and cook until the sauce is creamy and the pasta is al dente. Serve topped with more grated cheese, if desired.

⅓ cup plus 2 tablespoons extra-virgin olive oil

5 garlic cloves, smashed and peeled

3 (14-ounce) cans peeled cherry tomatoes or San Marzano tomatoes (see Cook's Note)

3 large full stems of basil

1 carrot, peeled and cut in half crosswise

½ pound Parmigiano-Reggiano rinds, cut into 3-inch pieces

1 teaspoon kosher salt, plus more as needed

1 pound penne rigate

½ cup freshly grated Parmigiano-Reggiano, plus more (optional) for serving

3 to 4 tablespoons unsalted butter

COOK'S NOTE: If you use the San Marzanos instead of cherry tomatoes, add another carrot for sweetness.

spaghetti with chianti and fava beans

YIELD:
SERVES 6

SERVE WITH:
**SHAVED ARTICHOKE AND
FENNEL SALAD
OLIVE OIL AND HONEY
PANNA COTTA**

This dish isn't all that hard or time-consuming to make, but it's a little extravagant for a weeknight because it uses a full bottle of Chianti. It's very reminiscent of Tuscany, where red table wine flows like water! The fun part of this recipe is the way the pasta becomes an amazing pinkish purple, but color aside, the wine gives the pasta a richness you can't get from plain water. Fava beans are a springtime specialty, but you can make this all year long if you substitute peas. Try this dish when you want to wow your friends.

1 (750 ml) bottle of Chianti or other full-bodied red wine

Kosher salt

1 pound spaghetti

2 tablespoons olive oil

¾ pound spicy Italian sausage, casings removed

1 shallot, chopped

1 garlic clove, minced

1 cup freshly grated Parmigiano-Reggiano

¼ cup mascarpone cheese, at room temperature

2 pounds fava beans, taken out of the pod, blanched, and peeled (see Cook's Note)

1 teaspoon chopped fresh rosemary

Pour the bottle of Chianti into a large pasta pot and add 2 quarts of water. Add a handful of salt and bring to a boil over high heat. Add the spaghetti and cook to just under al dente, about 8 minutes. Do not drain; you will need the pasta water for the sauce.

While the pasta is cooking, heat a large skillet over medium-high heat. Add the olive oil and sausage to the hot pan, and cook, breaking apart the sausage with the back of a wooden spoon. When the sausage is almost entirely cooked, about 4 minutes, add the shallot and garlic, and cook an additional 2 minutes, stirring often. Using tongs or a pasta fork, scoop the pasta directly into the pan with the sausage. Sprinkle with ¾ cup of the Parmigiano-Reggiano and toss with the tongs to combine. Add the mascarpone, fava beans, ¼ teaspoon salt, the rosemary, and about 1 cup of the pasta cooking water. Stir with a wooden spoon to combine, adding more pasta water as needed to form a sauce and coat the pasta. Serve sprinkled with the remaining ¼ cup Parmigiano-Reggiano.

COOK'S NOTE: To prepare the fava beans, remove the beans from their pods. Bring a pot of salted water to a boil. Fill a large bowl halfway with ice and cover the ice with water. Add the beans to the boiling water and blanch for 30 seconds. Drain well and plunge into the ice water to stop the cooking. Peel the white skin from the green shell bean and discard. The beans are now ready for use.

penne with pork ragu

YIELD:
SERVES 8

SERVE WITH:
**ANTIPASTI IN A JAR
WHITE CHOCOLATE
ORZO PUDDING**

This is quintessential Sunday supper fare. The pork shoulder becomes so succulent and falls apart. I have several friends who don't eat red meat, so this is my alternative to short-rib ragu, and though it's lighter, it's every bit as satisfying. You don't even need the pasta; I have been known to eat it straight from a bowl, with or without a piece of crusty bread. This feeds a crowd generously or makes two meals for a smaller group.

3 pounds pork shoulder roast, cut into large (1 × 3 × 3-inch) chunks

1½ tablespoons kosher salt, plus more as needed

¼ teaspoon freshly ground black pepper

2 to 3 tablespoons vegetable oil

2 medium Spanish onions, peeled, halved, and sliced thin tip to tip (approximately 4 cups)

5 garlic cloves, chopped

1 cup dry white wine

2 (6-inch) fresh rosemary sprigs

8 fresh thyme sprigs

1 bay leaf

½ cup low-sodium chicken broth

1 (28-ounce) can crushed tomatoes

1 (3-inch) piece of Parmigiano-Reggiano rind

Pinch of crushed red pepper flakes

¼ cup extra-virgin olive oil, plus more for drizzling

6 tablespoons freshly grated Parmigiano-Reggiano

1 pound penne pasta

Arugula, for garnish (optional)

Heat a Dutch oven over high heat. Dry the pieces of pork well and season them on all sides with 1 tablespoon of the salt and the pepper. Pour 2 tablespoons of the vegetable oil into the pan. Add the pork in batches, being careful not to crowd the pan. Brown the pieces on all sides, approximately 4 minutes per side. Remove the browned pork to a plate and continue to add and brown pieces until all the pork is seared.

Reduce the heat to medium. If the pan no longer has oil in it, add the last tablespoon of vegetable oil. Add all of the onions and season with the remaining ½ tablespoon salt and cook for about 8 minutes, stirring and scraping up the browned bits that have formed on the bottom of the pan. Add the chopped garlic and cook for another 2 to 3 minutes. Deglaze with the white wine, continuing to scrape up the bits from the bottom. Allow the wine to reduce until the pan is almost dry, 6 to 10 minutes more.

With a piece of butcher's twine, tie together the sprigs of rosemary and thyme with the bay leaf so they will be easier to remove later. Add the bundle to the pot, along with the chicken broth, crushed tomatoes, cheese rind, and red pepper flakes, and bring to a simmer. Add the pork back to the pot, pushing it down into the sauce. Reduce the heat to low, cover the pot, and simmer for 1 hour and 45 minutes, or until the pork is fork-tender.

Remove the pork from the pan and use two forks to shred it into bite-size pieces. Discard the herb bundle and cheese rind. Return the pork to the pot. Stir in the extra-virgin olive oil and 3 tablespoons of the grated Parmigiano-Reggiano. Keep warm over low heat.

Bring a large pot of salted water to a boil over high heat. Add the pasta and cook 1 to 2 minutes less than the package directions, approximately 12 minutes. Drain, reserving a cup of the cooking water, and add the pasta to the sauce, tossing to coat it evenly. Cook for the last 2 minutes in the sauce, adding a ladle of pasta water if needed to loosen the sauce. Top with the remaining 3 tablespoons Parmigiano-Reggiano and a drizzle of olive oil, if desired. Garnish with a few sprigs of arugula, if desired, and serve.

ziti stufati

Another impressive and delicious but labor-intensive dish Italians generally only undertake when there are extra hands around to help assemble it. My family made it every Sunday—along with pizza—and whenever I serve it, I'm flooded with memories of those wonderful meals.

YIELD:
SERVES 8

SERVE WITH:
**ROMAN SEAFOOD CHOWDER
FENNEL UPSIDE-DOWN CAKE**

Kosher salt

1 pound ziti rigate

FOR THE SAUCE

6 tablespoons extra-virgin olive oil

1 red onion, peeled and cut in half

1 garlic clove, smashed and peeled

1 carrot, peeled and grated

1 celery stalk, cut in half

½ teaspoon crushed red pepper flakes

1½ teaspoons kosher salt

2 (24.5-ounce) jars tomato puree, such as Mutti

1 (4-inch) piece of Parmigiano-Reggiano rind

5 fresh basil sprigs

1 cup whole-milk ricotta, at room temperature

FOR THE MEATBALLS

½ cup whole milk, at room temperature

1 large egg, beaten, at room temperature

1 cup stale bread (about 2 small slices of a rustic Italian loaf), crusts removed and insides torn into pieces

½ cup freshly grated Parmigiano-Reggiano

¼ cup fresh flat-leaf parsley, chopped

¾ teaspoon kosher salt

1 pound ground sirloin

Vegetable oil, for frying

FOR ASSEMBLY

2 large hard-boiled eggs, peeled and chopped

½ pound fresh mozzarella cheese, torn into 1-inch pieces

1 cup freshly grated Parmigiano-Reggiano

Bring a large pot of salted water to a boil over high heat. Fill a large bowl halfway with ice and cover the ice with cold water. Add the ziti to the boiling water and cook for 5 minutes. Drain well and plunge into the ice water to stop the cooking. Remove from the ice water when the pasta is chilled and drain again.

Heat a medium Dutch oven over medium-high heat. Add 3 table-spoons of the olive oil, the onion, garlic, carrot, celery, and red pepper flakes to the hot pan. Cook, stirring often, for 2 minutes, or

recipe continues »

until the carrots are beginning to soften. Season with ½ teaspoon of the salt and add the tomato puree. Rinse out the tomato jars with ⅓ cup water and add that to the pan as well. Add the cheese rind and basil, and stir to combine. Bring the sauce to a simmer. Reduce the heat to medium-low, partially cover the pan with the lid, and simmer for 40 minutes.

Remove the cheese rind, onion, celery, garlic, and basil sprigs, and discard. Season with the remaining 1 teaspoon salt and stir in the remaining 3 tablespoons olive oil. Add the ricotta and whisk to combine. Set aside.

In a medium bowl, whisk together the milk and egg. Stir in the bread and soak for 3 minutes, tearing the bread into small bits with your fingers. Add the Parmigiano-Reggiano, parsley, salt, and ground sirloin. Mix gently with your hands just until combined.

Heat a large skillet over medium heat. Add enough vegetable oil to come 1 inch up the side of the pan. When the oil is hot, roll the mixture into little meatballs, using about 1 teaspoon for each. Fry the balls in batches, cooking them for 3 minutes on each side, or until evenly browned. Do not overcrowd the pan while cooking the meatballs. Using a slotted spoon, remove the balls to a paper towel–lined baking sheet to drain. Continue until all the meatballs are browned.

Preheat the oven to 400°F.

Place the ziti in a large bowl. Add 3 to 4 cups of the sauce and toss well to coat the pasta with the sauce.

Ladle 1 cup of the sauce into a 9 × 13-inch baking dish and spread it out to cover the bottom. Add half the pasta, followed by half of the remaining sauce. Scatter three-quarters of the meatballs over the sauce and sprinkle with the chopped eggs, half the mozzarella, and ½ cup grated Parmigiano-Reggiano. Top with the remaining pasta, meatballs, and mozzarella. Cover with the remaining sauce and sprinkle with the last ½ cup Parmigiano-Reggiano.

Bake for 30 minutes, or until the top is lightly browned and the sauce is bubbling around the edges. Cool for 10 minutes before serving.

creamy lobster linguine

Whoever said "Bacon makes everything better" might have been thinking about this dish. The smoky bacon enhances the lobster and gives the dish sweetness. No sides needed, except maybe bread to sop up the sauce. Seafood sauces with tomato—like this—are popular all over the southern part of Italy.

YIELD:
SERVES 6

SERVE WITH:
ASPARAGUS WITH GRILLED MELON SALAD

Bring a very large pot of water to a boil. Add the lobsters, cover the pot, and boil the lobsters for 12 minutes. Use tongs to transfer the lobsters to a colander (or the sink) and drain. When cool enough to handle, remove the meat from the tail, claws, and knuckles. Cut the lobster meat in large bite-size pieces and set aside.

Heat a large straight-sided skillet over medium heat. Add the olive oil and bacon, and cook for 8 minutes, or until the bacon is beginning to crisp. Add the shallots, garlic, and red pepper flakes, and cook for an additional 3 minutes, until fragrant. Add the salt and tomato puree along with the cream, and stir to combine. Reduce the heat to low and simmer for 5 minutes.

Bring a large pot of salted water to a boil. Add the linguine and cook for 1 minute less than the package directions, about 10 minutes. Using tongs, remove the pasta from the water (reserving the pasta cooking water) and add it directly to the pan with the sauce. Sprinkle the Parmigiano-Reggiano directly on the naked pasta and then toss to coat in the sauce. Add up to 1 cup of pasta water, as needed, to loosen the sauce. Stir in the arugula, tarragon, basil, peas, and lobster, and simmer an additional minute, or until everything is heated through. Serve with additional Parmigiano-Reggiano, if desired.

2 (1½-pound) lobsters or ½ pound cooked lobster meat

3 tablespoons olive oil

2 slices bacon, chopped

3 shallots, minced

2 garlic cloves, chopped

¼ teaspoon crushed red pepper flakes

½ teaspoon kosher salt, plus more as needed

2 cups tomato puree

¼ cup heavy cream

1 pound linguine

¼ cup freshly grated Parmigiano-Reggiano, plus more (optional) for serving

1 cup baby arugula, coarsely chopped

¼ cup fresh tarragon leaves, coarsely chopped

½ cup fresh basil leaves, coarsely chopped

1 cup frozen peas, thawed

mushroom and asparagus farrotto

YIELD:
SERVES 4

SERVE WITH:
**PAN-ROASTED CLAMS
PEACH AND ALMOND CROSTATA**

Sunday dinner doesn't always need to be about a big piece of lamb, and sometimes it doesn't need to include meat at all! Cooking toothy farro, a grain related to wheat, as you would risotto makes a hearty dish that is cozy, warming, and full of flavor. These sturdy grains take a bit longer to cook than rice would, which makes this perfect for a slow weekend afternoon.

2 leeks, white and tender green parts only

4 tablespoons extra-virgin olive oil

10 ounces cremini or mixed mushrooms, sliced

2 garlic cloves, smashed and peeled

½ teaspoon kosher salt

1 cup pearled farro, rinsed and drained

1 cup dry white wine

3 cups low-sodium chicken or vegetable broth

½ cup freshly grated Pecorino Romano cheese

⅔ cup freshly grated Parmigiano-Reggiano, plus more (optional) for serving

¼ cup (½ stick) unsalted butter

½ pound asparagus, trimmed and sliced into thin rounds

Halve the trimmed leeks lengthwise, then cut them crosswise into half-moons. Rinse under running water; drain well.

Heat a 3½-quart pan over medium-high heat. Add 2 tablespoons of the olive oil and heat another 30 seconds. Add the mushrooms to the pan and cook, stirring often, for 8 to 10 minutes, or until they are golden brown and all of the water has cooked out. Using a slotted spoon, remove the mushrooms to a plate. Add the remaining 2 tablespoons oil and the leeks. Reduce the heat to medium and cook the leeks, stirring often, until soft and fragrant, about 3 minutes. Add the garlic and salt, and cook an additional minute.

Add the farro to the pan and stir to coat the grains in the oil and toast them slightly; this will take another 2 to 3 minutes. Stir in the wine and cook, stirring occasionally, until it is almost completely absorbed; this will take about 8 minutes. Add 1 cup of the broth, stir, and cook until it has been absorbed by the grain. Continue adding broth in 1-cup increments and cooking it down until it's almost absorbed between additions. Stir the farro often to help create a creamy texture. This will take about 45 minutes to complete.

When the farro is tender and almost all of the liquid has been absorbed, stir in the cheeses and butter. Continue to stir until the mixture is creamy. Fold in the asparagus and mushrooms, and heat for another 2 minutes to cook the asparagus. Serve with more grated Parmigiano-Reggiano, if desired.

barolo-braised short ribs

In Tuscany this dish is as common as pot roast is in the United States and would be prepared with Barolo, a wine made from the region's Nebbiolo grapes. However, you can substitute any full-bodied wine; Chianti, Syrah, and Zinfandel will all work. The salad topping adds a bit of freshness and crunch to the long-cooked meat that is really lovely. If you have leftovers (and you won't have as much as you think), they are great with eggs in the morning or shredded and served over pasta. This goes very well with creamy polenta or risotto.

YIELD:
SERVES 4 TO 6

SERVE WITH:
CHEESY MASHED POTATOES
WILTED BABY KALE
WHITE CHOCOLATE ORZO
PUDDING

FOR THE SHORT RIBS

4 fresh thyme sprigs

2 fresh rosemary sprigs

1 bay leaf

3 tablespoons olive oil

5 pounds bone-in beef short ribs, cut into 4-inch pieces

2½ teaspoons kosher salt

½ cup all-purpose flour

1 red onion, finely chopped

1 celery stalk, finely chopped

2 carrots, peeled and finely chopped

¼ cup tomato paste

1 (750 ml) bottle of Barolo or Nebbiolo wine

2 cups low-sodium beef broth

1 (3-inch) piece of Parmigiano-Reggiano rind

FOR THE FENNEL SALAD

1 fennel bulb, stalks removed, shaved thin on a mandoline

1 cup baby arugula, roughly chopped

1 teaspoon fresh lemon juice

2 teaspoons olive oil

¼ teaspoon kosher salt

Preheat the oven to 325°F. Using butcher's twine, tie the herb sprigs and bay leaf together in a bundle and set it aside.

Heat the olive oil in a Dutch oven over medium-high heat. Dry the short ribs well with paper towels and season them evenly with 2 teaspoons of the salt. Dredge each rib in the flour, shaking off the excess, and place them in the hot pan. Sear the meat until evenly browned on all sides, about 12 minutes total. Remove the meat to a plate.

recipe continues »

To the same pan, add the onion, celery, and carrots. Season with the remaining ½ teaspoon salt and cook, stirring often and scraping the bottom of the pan, for 4 minutes, or until the vegetables are starting to soften and brown slightly. Add the tomato paste and stir for an additional 3 minutes to caramelize; it will turn a deep red color. Add the wine and bring it to a simmer, scraping up the brown bits from the bottom of the pan. Simmer for 5 minutes, or until the wine is slightly reduced. Add the broth, herb bundle, and cheese rind, and return to a simmer. Nestle the meat in the pan, adding any juices that accumulated on the plate. Cover the pot and place it in the oven for approximately 2½ hours, or until the meat is fork-tender. Remove the ribs to a plate. Skim the fat off the surface and discard it, along with the herb bundle and cheese rind. Return the meat to the sauce and spoon some sauce over the ribs to coat them.

In a medium bowl toss together the shaved fennel, arugula, lemon juice, olive oil, and salt.

Serve each short rib with a spoonful of sauce and top with some of the fennel salad.

mementos

One thing Americans visiting Italy are always struck by is the way you are surrounded by antiquity everywhere you go. In downtown Rome, ongoing excavations of centuries-old artifacts are an everyday sight, and antiques shops are a fun way to bring some of this old-world flavor home with you. I especially like collecting serving pieces and copper pots, which just become more burnished and beautiful with age. A copper mold, like those used to make the Sartu di Riso (page 159), would be a beautiful kitchen decoration between uses, and dessert spoons and forks—mismatched designs is stylishly boho—make any birthday celebration more special. A tiny sterling salt spoon is an elegant and reasonably priced way to add a little old-world charm to your dinner table, and it is a lot easier to tuck into your luggage than a souvenir bottle of limoncello. Any of these will be conversation pieces you'll enjoy for years to come.

lamb osso buco

Veal osso buco is more familiar to American cooks, but in Italy, lamb shanks are often prepared the same way. The broth is a bit lighter and herbier, but it's still a hearty wintertime dish. The parsley and lemon zest add a bright note at the end. Serve it over polenta or a small pasta like orzo, or simply with crusty bread. You'll need to have the butcher cut the whole shanks into portions for you.

YIELD:
SERVES 4

SERVE WITH:
SMOKED SCAMORZA, SPINACH, AND PANCETTA PIZZA
CREAMY POLENTA WITH SPINACH
CHIANTI AFFOGATO

Heat the oil in a large Dutch oven over medium-high heat. Dry the lamb pieces very well and season with 1 teaspoon of the salt. Dredge each piece in the flour, shaking off the excess. Add the lamb to the pan and sear on all sides until deep golden brown; this will take 8 to 10 minutes. Remove the seared lamb to a plate.

Add the onion, garlic, carrot, and celery to the pan, and season with the remaining ½ teaspoon salt. Cook for about 3 minutes, until the vegetables are beginning to brown and the mixture is fragrant. Add the tomato paste and cook, stirring often, for about 2 minutes to caramelize the paste. Stir in the white wine and bring to a simmer, scraping the bottom of the pan to loosen any browned bits. Reduce the heat to medium and simmer for 3 minutes.

Add the chicken broth, rosemary, thyme, and bay leaf to the pan and stir to combine. Nestle the lamb pieces back in the pan so they are partially covered with liquid. Cover the pan, reduce the heat to low, and cook for 2 hours, or until the lamb is soft and tender.

Use tongs to remove the meat to a plate and keep warm. Skim the fat from the surface of the sauce and discard the herb sprigs and bay leaf. Return the meat to the sauce and serve directly from the pot, sprinkling each serving with parsley and lemon zest.

3 tablespoons vegetable oil

4 pounds lamb shank, cut in 2-inch lengths (about 4 large shanks)

1½ teaspoons kosher salt

⅓ cup all-purpose flour

1 onion, chopped

3 garlic cloves, smashed and peeled

1 large carrot, peeled and diced into ⅓-inch pieces

2 celery stalks, chopped into ⅓-inch pieces

¼ cup tomato paste

1 cup dry white wine

3 cups low-sodium chicken broth

1 fresh rosemary sprig

3 fresh thyme sprigs

1 bay leaf

2 tablespoons chopped fresh flat-leaf parsley

1 teaspoon grated lemon zest

italian springtime lamb

A whole leg of lamb—boned, stuffed, rolled, and roasted—is the perfect dish for a large gathering or holiday meal. It looks spectacular when it's sliced, and it serves a big group. Don't try to carve it too thin or the filling will fall out; ¾ inch is ideal. Definitely let this dish rest before you slice it, because it won't be fully cooked without that resting period. Leftovers also make yummy sandwiches the next day.

YIELD:
SERVES 8 TO 10

SERVE WITH:
**CRAB ARANCINI
WHITE BEANS AND TUSCAN KALE
MASCARPONE CANNOLI
CHEESECAKE**

FOR THE LAMB

1 (5-pound) trimmed and boned leg of lamb, butterflied

3 tablespoons olive oil

6 garlic cloves, minced

4 fresh rosemary sprigs, leaves removed and chopped

¼ teaspoon crushed red pepper flakes

½ cup chopped walnuts

1 (5-ounce) container baby spinach leaves, roughly chopped

1½ teaspoons kosher salt

¾ cup raisins

½ teaspoon freshly ground black pepper

½ cup whole-grain mustard

FOR THE BREAD-CRUMB GREMOLATA

1 tablespoon olive oil

⅓ cup panko bread crumbs

⅓ cup coarsely chopped fresh flat-leaf parsley

1 teaspoon grated lemon zest

¼ teaspoon crushed red pepper flakes

⅛ teaspoon kosher salt

Remove the leg of lamb from the refrigerator 30 minutes before cooking.

In a large sauté pan, warm 2 tablespoons of the olive oil over medium-high heat. Add the garlic, rosemary, red pepper flakes, and walnuts, toasting them until fragrant and beginning to brown, 3 to 4 minutes. Add the chopped spinach and ½ teaspoon of salt, and cook until wilted. Stir in the raisins.

Preheat the oven to 350°F.

Lay the leg of lamb flat on a board in front of you, boned-side up. If it is very thick or uneven, pound it gently to an even 1-inch

recipe continues »

thickness using a small skillet or a rolling pin. Sprinkle the surface with ½ teaspoon of the salt and the pepper. Spread the mustard evenly over the lamb. Distribute the spinach mixture evenly over the mustard. Starting from one long side, roll the leg with the filling inside, pinwheel-style, and tie it every 2 inches with butcher's twine so it maintains the shape of the leg. Season the outside with the remaining ½ teaspoon salt.

Wipe out the sauté pan and add the remaining tablespoon of olive oil. Place the pan over high heat and allow the pan and oil to get hot. Place the roast, fat-side down, in the pan and sear on all sides until golden brown all over, about 2 minutes per side. Place the roast on a rimmed baking sheet or in a roasting pan and roast for 1 hour and 15 minutes, or until an instant-read thermometer registers 125°F. Remove the roast to a cutting board and let it rest for 30 minutes.

WHILE THE LAMB IS ROASTING, PREPARE THE GREMOLATA: In a small sauté pan, heat the olive oil over medium-high heat. Add the panko and toast, stirring regularly, until the bread crumbs are an even golden brown, 3 to 4 minutes. Add the parsley, lemon zest, red pepper flakes, and salt to the warm bread crumbs. Toss and set aside to let the flavors mingle.

Remove twine, cut the lamb into generous slices and serve with a sprinkling of the bread-crumb gremolata.

marinated bistecca fiorentina

A big, thick steak like this is a real treat; served with a plate of pasta it's the quintessential Sunday dinner. It's the herb char on the steak that makes it irresistible, and the squeeze of lemon on the hot meat wakes up all the herbal notes and brightens the char flavor as it enters your mouth. Italians typically slice it and serve it over a bed of arugula for everyone to share, making one steak go a long way.

YIELD:
SERVES 2 TO 4

SERVE WITH:
**WARM MUSHROOM SALAD
FIORENTINA
ROASTED SQUASH WITH
CHERRIES AND PISTACHIOS**

Place the steak on a plate or rimmed baking sheet. Rub the steak all over with the garlic cloves. Sprinkle the steak evenly with the chopped rosemary, chopped thyme, and lemon zest, and drizzle with the olive oil. Rub the mixture into the meat and allow it to sit at room temperature for 30 minutes.

Prepare your grill or heat a grill pan over medium-high heat. Preheat your oven to 500°F and set a wire rack inside a rimmed baking sheet.

Season the steak evenly on both sides with the kosher salt. Place the steak on the grill and cook on each side for 5 minutes, or until nicely seared all around. If you like, you can char the lemon half on the grill at the same time you are searing the steak for even more grilled goodness.

Transfer the steak to the rack on the baking sheet and roast in the oven for an additional 15 minutes, flipping halfway through, or until an instant-read thermometer inserted in the middle of the steak registers 120°F. Remove the steak to a plate, squeeze the ½ lemon over the steak, and allow it to rest for 10 minutes before slicing and finishing it with a sprinkling of coarse salt.

1 (2-pound) rib-eye steak, about 2 inches thick

2 garlic cloves, smashed

½ teaspoon chopped fresh rosemary

¼ teaspoon chopped fresh thyme

½ teaspoon grated lemon zest (from ½ lemon)

2 tablespoons olive oil

1 teaspoon kosher salt

½ lemon

½ teaspoon coarse salt, for finishing

tricolore stuffed pork

YIELD:
SERVES 8

SERVE WITH:
**SAVORY CROSTATA
CREAMY SWEET CORN WITH
PANCETTA
POUND CAKE WITH
LIMONCELLO ZABAGLIONE**

When you slice this roast, you will see the colors of the Italian flag: white cheese, red peppers, and green spinach. All the work is in the prep; once you're done filling and tying the pork loin, the rest is just roasting, leaving you with plenty of time to make your sides. When I make a pork dish, I always like to serve it with something that is on the creamier side to keep the pork moist.

1 onion

1 (5-pound) boneless pork loin, butterflied (see Cook's Note)

1¼ teaspoons kosher salt

10 slices provolone picante cheese

4 whole jarred roasted red peppers

2 cups baby spinach

4 fresh rosemary sprigs

2 cups low-sodium chicken broth

2 tablespoons olive oil

COOK'S NOTE: To butterfly the pork loin, place it perpendicular to you on a cutting board. Holding a large chef's knife, make a long, smooth slit into the lower third of the loin, almost but not completely through to the other side. Open the loin with the cut surface up. Repeat the process one more time, cutting almost all the way through the center of the thicker portion of the pork and opening it up to create a large, evenly thin piece of meat.

Preheat the oven to 425°F. Peel the onion and slice it crosswise into 4 rounds. Place it in a 9 × 13-inch baking dish and set aside.

Using the tip of a sharp knife, score the fat on the top of the loin in a diamond pattern, making the cuts about ¼ inch deep. Unroll the pork loin so it is completely flat, fat-side down. Season the inside with ½ teaspoon salt. Lay the provolone slices on the pork, overlapping them slightly. Open the peppers so they lie flat. Tear or cut them in half so you are left with 8 triangles. Arrange the peppers on the cheese, fitting them together like a puzzle. Spread the spinach evenly over the peppers. Beginning at one side edge, roll the pork loin back into its original shape, with the fat on top, and tie it in 4 places using butcher's twine.

Season the roast all over with the remaining ¾ teaspoon salt. Set the pork in the baking dish on the bed of onions. Scatter the rosemary sprigs around it and pour the broth into the pan. Drizzle the pork with the olive oil. Roast for about 50 minutes, or until the top is golden brown.

Baste the pork with the pan juices and reduce the heat to 375°F. Roast approximately 40 minutes longer, or until an instant-read thermometer inserted in the center registers 150°F. Remove from the oven and allow the pork to rest for 15 minutes before slicing. Strain the pan juices and serve alongside the pork.

veal saltimbocca milanese-style

YIELD:
SERVES 2

SERVE WITH:
**SHAVED ARTICHOKE AND
FENNEL SALAD
MASCARPONE SORBETTO WITH
ROSEMARY HONEY**

Here's a twofer, a mash-up of two beloved Italian dishes: veal saltimbocca and chicken Milanese. It's crispy, gooey, and decadent, and one chop will really feed two people for a romantic dinner. It's important to pound the veal chop into a flat, even surface in order to get it nice and crispy.

1 (12-ounce) bone-in veal rib chop

3 thin slices fontina cheese (about 1 ounce)

6 small fresh sage leaves

2 thin slices prosciutto di San Daniele

½ cup all-purpose flour

2 large eggs, beaten

¾ cup panko bread crumbs

¾ teaspoon kosher salt

¼ teaspoon freshly ground black pepper

⅓ cup extra-virgin olive oil

Parmigiano-Reggiano shavings (optional)

Fried sage (optional)

Grilled lemon (optional)

Using a sharp, thin knife, cut a horizontal slit into the side of the veal chop almost to the bone, forming a 3-inch-deep pocket. Cover the chop with a piece of plastic wrap. Using the flat side of a meat mallet or a small heavy skillet, gently pound the chop until it is about ⅓ inch thick. Discard the plastic wrap. Stuff 1 piece of the fontina cheese into the veal pocket and close the meat around it. Place 3 small sage leaves on one side of the chop. Cover the sage leaves with another piece of cheese and follow that with a slice of prosciutto. Turn over the chop and repeat with the remaining sage, cheese, and prosciutto.

Place the flour, beaten egg, and panko in 3 separate shallow dishes, and season each of them with ¼ teaspoon of the salt and the pepper. Dredge both sides of the veal chop in the flour and shake off the excess. Dip the chop into the beaten egg and then into the panko, packing the bread crumbs onto the chop to help them stick.

Preheat the oven to 400°F.

In a medium skillet, heat the olive oil over medium-high heat. Add the chop and cook for about 2 minutes, or until the bread crumbs on the first side are golden brown. Carefully flip the chop and brown the second side. Transfer the chop to a baking sheet and place it in the oven for 8 to 10 minutes, or until an instant-read thermometer inserted horizontally into the side of the chop registers 155°F.

Serve topped with Parmigiano-Reggiano shavings and fried sage.

grilled chicken involtini

Involtini means "rolled," and you'll find rolled and stuffed dishes like these throughout northern Italy. There, cooks use tougher cuts of beef, simmering them in sauce until tender; I've adapted this technique for the grill using fast-cooking chicken cutlets to simplify things and make cleanup easier. The crunchy and cheesy bites that ooze out of the sides are irresistible. Most kids go crazy for this, but it has sophisticated flavors adults will enjoy, too.

YIELD:
SERVES 4 TO 6

SERVE WITH:
**CHARRED BROCCOLI RABE
GRILLED ARTICHOKE WITH
ANCHOVY MAYONNAISE**

Preheat a grill to medium-high heat. Move the coals to one side so that you can cook the chicken over indirect heat.

MAKE THE SAUCE: In a small bowl, stir together the parsley, lemon zest, olive oil, and salt. Set aside.

PREPARE THE INVOLTINI: In a separate small bowl, mix the oregano, salt, and red pepper flakes together. Lay a chicken cutlet lengthwise on your work surface and season it all over with the salt mixture. Place a piece of prosciutto on top, followed by a piece of provolone folded in half. Top with 1 sun-dried tomato. Roll the cutlet, enclosing the fillings, and secure with 2 parallel skewers. Repeat with the remaining ingredients, placing 2 rolls on each pair of skewers for easy flipping.

Drizzle the rolls with the olive oil and place them on the grill directly over the coals. Sear the chicken on both sides for 10 minutes, or until golden brown, flipping as needed. Move the skewers away from the hot coals, cover the grill, and cook with indirect heat for an additional 10 minutes, or until cooked through, turning once. Transfer to a platter and allow to rest for 5 minutes.

Remove the skewers from the involtini, slice, and serve drizzled with the sauce.

FOR THE SAUCE

¼ cup chopped fresh flat-leaf parsley

1 teaspoon grated lemon zest (from ½ lemon)

⅓ cup extra-virgin olive oil

¼ teaspoon kosher salt

FOR THE INVOLTINI

¼ teaspoon dried oregano

¾ teaspoon kosher salt

¼ teaspoon crushed red pepper flakes

8 chicken breast cutlets

8 thin slices prosciutto di Parma

8 slices provolone picante cheese

8 oil-packed sun-dried tomatoes

1 tablespoon extra-virgin olive oil

hazelnut chicken

YIELD:
SERVES 4

SERVE WITH:
ROASTED PARMIGIANO-
REGGIANO POTATOES
ANGEL FOOD CAKE WITH
CHOCOLATE-HAZELNUT
FROSTING

Dried fruit and nuts (especially hazelnuts) make their way into many dishes in Tuscany, and they create a great flavorful sauce for this braised chicken. The hazelnut liqueur adds sweetness and nuttiness, while the balsamic adds tang. It's a simple way to transform a one-pot chicken dish into something that seems a bit more special and sophisticated.

1 (4-pound) chicken, cut into 8 serving pieces

1½ teaspoons kosher salt

2 tablespoons olive oil

1 onion, chopped

2 carrots, peeled and chopped

2 celery stalks, chopped

3 tablespoons hazelnut liqueur, such as Frangelico

2 tablespoons balsamic vinegar

2 cups low-sodium chicken broth

1 cup Cerignola olives that have been crushed with the side of a chef's knife

½ cup dried figs, quartered

3 fresh oregano sprigs

½ cup chopped skinless hazelnuts

¼ cup fresh flat-leaf parsley leaves, chopped

Using paper towels, dry the chicken pieces well. Season on all sides with the salt. Heat a 5½-quart braising pan or Dutch oven over medium-high heat. Add the olive oil to the pan and heat for another minute, until the oil dances.

Add the chicken to the hot pan, skin-side down, and cook for about 4 minutes, or until the skin is golden brown and the chicken releases easily from the pan. Flip the chicken and sear the other side for 4 minutes, or until nicely browned. Remove the chicken to a plate and set aside.

To the hot pan, add the onion, carrots, and celery. Cook, stirring often with a wooden spoon, for about 3 minutes, or until the vegetables are fragrant and beginning to soften. Add the hazelnut liqueur and vinegar to the pan, and scrape up any brown bits from the bottom of the pan. Simmer until the liquid is reduced by half, 1 or 2 minutes. Stir in the chicken broth, olives, figs, and oregano. Nestle the chicken pieces into the liquid, skin-side down, and cover the pan. Simmer for 30 minutes, turning the chicken pieces skin-side up after 15 minutes.

Remove the braised chicken to a clean platter to rest and simmer the sauce, uncovered, for an additional 5 minutes to reduce slightly. Discard the oregano sprigs. Pour the sauce over the chicken and sprinkle with the hazelnuts and parsley.

grilled scallops with prosciutto and basil

My friend Pam makes these pretty skewers on the grill at her beach house on Long Island. Pink peppercorns make them beautiful and summery—as if you're eating a spicy rose petal. You could serve this with (or atop) an arugula salad. Add a squeeze of juice from a grilled lemon half if you like.

YIELD:
SERVES 4

SERVE WITH:
GRILLED TREVISO WITH CITRUS BAGNA CAUDA
ASPARAGUS SALAD WITH GRILLED MELON

Preheat a grill pan over medium-high heat.

Cut the prosciutto slices in half lengthwise to make 12 long strips. Season the scallops evenly with the salt. Place 1 basil leaf at the end of a strip of prosciutto, folding it in half lengthwise, if necessary. Place a scallop on its side on top of the basil and carefully roll the scallop inside the basil and prosciutto. Secure with a toothpick or skewer. Repeat with the remaining ingredients.

Drizzle the scallops with the olive oil. Place the scallops on the heated grill pan, pressing down gently to make sure the scallops make direct contact with the hot surface. Grill for 2 to 3 minutes per side, or until nice grill marks form and the scallops are just warm in the center (see Cook's Note). Remove the scallops to a plate and sprinkle with the pink peppercorns.

6 thin slices prosciutto di San Daniele

12 large sea scallops

¼ teaspoon kosher salt

12 fresh basil leaves

1 tablespoon olive oil

½ teaspoon crushed pink peppercorns

COOK'S NOTE: To check if the scallops are done, simply insert a thin metal cake tester into the center and leave it there for 10 seconds. Remove and place the metal against the skin beneath your lower lip. If the tester feels warm, the scallop is done.

italian barbecued shrimp

Italians like to grill, but tomato-based American-style barbecue sauce has never really taken hold there. This recipe is more like Italy—light and herby—with the same smoky, grilled flavor. There's nothing very complicated about this recipe but the sophisticated flavors are perfect for a weekend gathering indoors or out.

YIELD:
SERVES 4

SERVE WITH:
**BURRATA WITH NECTARINES
AND CORN
SAUSAGE AND BROCCOLI PIZZA
BLACK-AND-WHITE BROWNIE
ICE CREAM CAKE**

In a medium bowl, stir together the brown sugar, salt, paprika, oregano, fennel seed, and black pepper. Add the shrimp and toss to coat well. Cover with plastic wrap and refrigerate for about an hour.

Preheat a grill pan over medium heat.

Toss the marinated shrimp with the olive oil and place on the heated grill pan. Grill for about 3 minutes on each side, or until browned and opaque all the way through. Serve warm or at room temperature.

2 tablespoons packed light brown sugar

1 teaspoon kosher salt

1 teaspoon hot smoked paprika

1 teaspoon dried oregano

½ teaspoon ground fennel seed (see Cook's Note)

¼ teaspoon freshly ground black pepper

1 pound large shrimp, peeled and deveined

1 tablespoon olive oil

COOK'S NOTE: For the best flavor, buy whole fennel seeds and grind them yourself. You can crush the seeds with a mortar and pestle, whir them in a clean coffee grinder, or just chop them as finely as possible with a heavy knife.

slow-roasted salmon

YIELD:
SERVES 6

SERVE WITH:
**WARM MUSHROOM SALAD
ROASTED SQUASH WITH
CHERRIES AND PISTACHIOS**

If you want a dish with the impact of a whole fish but don't love the idea of cooking anything with its head on, this is the perfect solution. A gentle, slow roasting ensures that the fish doesn't dry out. The mustard and spices create a tasty crust that both perfumes the flesh and adds a nice textural counterpoint to the buttery salmon. It's a true showpiece that I make for springtime celebrations, because it's festive and vibrantly colored but not as heavy as ham or leg of lamb.

1 fennel bulb with stalks

1 tablespoon extra-virgin olive oil, plus more for drizzling

1 (4-pound) skin-on side of salmon, pin bones removed (see Cook's Notes)

¾ teaspoon kosher salt

¼ cup whole-grain mustard

2½ teaspoons coriander seeds, toasted and crushed (see Cook's Notes)

3 teaspoons fennel seeds, toasted and crushed (see Cook's Notes)

Preheat the oven to 300°F.

Trim the stalks from the fennel bulb, reserving the leafy fronds for garnish. Thinly slice the bulb crosswise.

Arrange the sliced fennel down the middle of a rimmed baking sheet and drizzle with the olive oil. Place the salmon, skin-side down, on top of the fennel and season it with the salt. Spread the mustard evenly over the salmon flesh and sprinkle with the coriander and fennel seeds. Press gently to help the crushed seeds adhere.

Roast for about 1 hour, or until a fork easily pierces the thickest part of the fish and the flesh flakes. Carefully transfer the salmon to a serving platter, leaving the fennel behind. Sprinkle the salmon with the reserved fennel fronds and drizzle with olive oil.

COOK'S NOTES: If you are not certain whether the pin bones have been removed, gently run your fingers over the surface of the fillet. If you feel the ends of the soft, white pin bones protruding, use a pair of sturdy tweezers or your fingers to gently extract them, trying to rip the flesh as little as possible. You can also ask your fishmonger to do this for you.

To toast the spices, place the seeds separately in a small dry skillet over medium heat. Heat them, stirring often, for 2 to 3 minutes, or until fragrant and starting to color. Transfer to a plate to cool completely, then grind (together is fine) using a mortar and pestle or a clean coffee grinder.

whole roasted fish

Don't be intimidated by the idea of cooking a whole fish. Not only is it very easy to do, but you are much less likely to overcook the fish this way and it will look quite elegant. In Italy this would be made with branzino, so feel free to substitute that, a whole black sea bass, snapper, or any other mild white fish you can find (or catch!).

YIELD:
SERVES 2

SERVE WITH:
SPAGHETTI WITH CHIANTI AND
FAVA BEANS
SAUTEÉD BABY KALE
CHOCOLATE CHERRY
SHORTBREAD COOKIES AND
MOSCATO

Position one oven rack in the top third of the oven. Preheat the oven to 400°F.

Dry the fish very well inside and out with paper towels. Score the skin twice on each side of the fish. Season the fish inside and out with 1½ teaspoons of the salt. Stuff the cavity of the fish with the rosemary, oregano, and orange slices. Close the belly around the filling.

On a rimmed baking sheet, toss the bell peppers with the olives, onion, remaining ½ teaspoon salt, the red pepper flakes, and 1 tablespoon of the olive oil. Place the fish in the middle of the vegetables and rub the outside with the remaining tablespoon oil. Roast for 25 to 30 minutes, or until the fish is cooked through and tender when pierced with a fork.

To fillet the fish, use a butter knife to cut the fish in half down to the central spine. Following the rib bones with the knife held horizontally, cut to the right to free half the fillet, then repeat to the left. Use a spatula to transfer both half fillets to a plate, then lift off and discard the bones, starting from the tail. Divide and plate the remaining fish. Serve the fillets with the spicy roasted pepper mixture.

1 whole red snapper (about 1½ pounds), cleaned, gutted, and fins removed, or any other mild white fish

2 teaspoons kosher salt

4 fresh rosemary sprigs

3 fresh oregano sprigs

½ orange, sliced (about 3 slices)

1 red bell pepper, cored, seeded, and cut into ½-inch strips

1 orange bell pepper, cored, seeded, and cut into ½-inch strips

½ cup pitted kalamata olives

½ red onion, cut into thin strips

½ teaspoon crushed red pepper flakes

2 tablespoons olive oil

ENDIVE, PANCETTA, AND
TOMATO SALAD

ASPARAGUS WITH
GRILLED MELON SALAD

SHAVED ARTICHOKE AND
FENNEL SALAD

CHOPPED ROMAINE AND
RADICCHIO SALAD

ITALIAN CARROT SALAD

TOMATO, AVOCADO, AND
ESCAROLE SALAD

WILTED BABY KALE

WARM MUSHROOM
SALAD FIORENTINA

ZUCCHINI SOTTOLIO

GRILLED TREVISO WITH
CITRUS BAGNA CAUDA

ROASTED SQUASH
AGRODOLCE

CHARRED BROCCOLI
RABE

CREAMY SWEET CORN
WITH PANCETTA

WHITE BEANS AND
TUSCAN KALE

ROASTED PARMIGIANO-
REGGIANO POTATOES

CHEESY MASHED
POTATOES

CREAMY POLENTA WITH
SPINACH

ROASTED SQUASH
WITH CHERRIES AND
PISTACHIOS

sides

Sides can seem like an afterthought, just something to put on the plate beside the main event, but these days, everyone is eating more vegetables, and that's a very good thing! Unless I'm serving pasta, I always make either a potato or grain dish or a vegetable to go with dinner, and usually both. In fact, I am very happy with two or three of these sides and no entrée at all! I wanted to come up with simple but flavorful side options that will give vegetables the respect they are due as nutritional powerhouses that also bring lots of color to our plates. That said, none of these will take much time to put together, and I promise that once you have made them a few times, you won't need to look at the recipe anymore.

endive, pancetta, and tomato salad

This is one of those simple yet unique salads that is a great accompaniment to almost anything. Coriander seeds warm the salad, giving it a wonderful aroma and flavor. A bit of pancetta lends body, crunch, and bacon-y goodness.

YIELD:
SERVES 4

SERVE WITH:
SPICY SAUSAGE AND ESCAROLE SOUP

Preheat the oven to 350°F.

Lay the pancetta slices on a rimmed baking sheet. Cook for about 10 minutes, or until deep brown and crisp. Drain on a paper towel–lined plate.

In a medium bowl, whisk together the mustard, vinegar, olive oil, and salt. Add the tomatoes, endives, and crushed coriander seeds, and toss gently to coat. Break the pancetta into 1- to 2-inch pieces and toss with the salad. Divide the dressed salad among 4 salad plates and sprinkle with the Parmigiano-Reggiano. Serve immediately.

6 thin slices pancetta

1 tablespoon whole-grain mustard

1 tablespoon white wine vinegar

2 tablespoons extra-virgin olive oil

¼ teaspoon kosher salt

2 cups cherry tomatoes, halved

2 Belgian endives, trimmed and cut in ¾-inch pieces

1 teaspoon coriander seeds, toasted and crushed (see Cook's Note)

1 cup freshly grated Parmigiano-Reggiano

COOK'S NOTE: To toast the coriander seeds, heat them in a dry skillet over medium heat just until fragrant, about 2 minutes. Immediately remove from the pan. When completely cool, use a mortar and pestle or the bottom of a heavy skillet to crush the seeds.

asparagus with grilled melon salad

YIELD:
SERVES 4

SERVE WITH:
FENNEL GRATIN PIZZETTE

This dish always makes me smile. First of all, the color is spectacular, and the combination of asparagus and melon reminds me of spring. If you've never cooked fruit on the grill, you should try it. Grilling melon intensifies its sweetness and caramelizes the sugars on the surface. I promise it will impress your friends, and everyone will want to make it. I poach the asparagus in butter so it's super tender and decadent—a nod to Florence and Tuscany, where this is common practice.

½ small cantaloupe, peeled, seeds removed, and cut in ½-inch slices

1 tablespoon olive oil

1 cup cherry tomatoes, quartered

1 tablespoon chopped fresh mint

¾ teaspoon kosher salt

1 teaspoon Calabrian chile paste

2 teaspoons fresh lime juice

½ cup (1 stick) unsalted butter, chilled

2 fresh thyme sprigs

1 pound medium-thick asparagus, trimmed

Ricotta salata cheese, shaved with a vegetable peeler (optional)

Preheat a grill over medium-high heat.

Drizzle the cantaloupe with the olive oil and place the slices on the grill. Grill the slices, without moving them, for about 30 seconds, or until browned on the first side. Flip the melon slices and grill on the other side for an additional 30 seconds. Remove to a cutting board to cool slightly.

Cut the melon slices into ½-inch pieces and place them in a medium bowl. Add the tomatoes, mint, ¼ teaspoon of the salt, the chile paste, and lime juice. Mix well and set aside to let the flavors mingle.

Meanwhile, heat 5 tablespoons of water in a large skillet over medium heat. Cut the butter into 8 pieces. When bubbles just start rising to the water's surface, begin adding the butter to the pan, 1 piece at a time, whisking constantly to form an emulsion. When all the butter is incorporated, reduce the heat to medium-low to keep the temperature just below a simmer. Add the thyme and the remaining ½ teaspoon salt, and swirl the pan to combine. Add the asparagus to the pan and toss gently to coat it in the butter.

Cover the pan and cook for 5 minutes, or until the asparagus is tender all the way through when pierced with the tip of a sharp knife. Remove the asparagus to a platter and spoon the melon salad on top. Scatter a few shavings of ricotta salata over the salad, if desired.

shaved artichoke and fennel salad

YIELD:
SERVES 4

SERVE WITH:
MUSSELS IN WHITE WINE

Artichokes aren't usually a vegetable you think of eating raw, because the leaves are just too fibrous unless they are cooked. The tender heart, though—subtle, crunchy, and delicious—is a different story. During artichoke season, you will find this on the menu of every restaurant in Italy, and the combination of the thinly sliced vegetables with just a little lemon juice, olive oil, and salt is phenomenal.

1½ tablespoons lemon juice

2 tablespoons extra-virgin olive oil

1½ cups baby arugula

5 baby artichokes, trimmed and thinly sliced lengthwise with a mandoline (see Cook's Note)

1 fennel bulb, stalks removed, sliced thin

½ teaspoon kosher salt

⅛ teaspoon freshly ground black pepper

½ cup Parmigiano-Reggiano shavings

In a small bowl, whisk together the lemon juice and olive oil. Place the arugula in a separate medium bowl. Spoon a small amount of dressing onto the arugula and toss to coat. Spread the arugula on a large plate and set aside.

In a large bowl, combine the sliced artichokes, fennel, remaining dressing, salt, and pepper. Mix well to coat. Mound the artichoke mixture on top of the arugula. Sprinkle with the Parmigiano-Reggiano shavings and serve.

COOK'S NOTE: The key to this elegant salad is using only the most tender part of the artichoke; you must get all the way down to the pale green core before slicing. Even with baby artichokes, you will need to be merciless about discarding the outer leaves, and that kills me because there's really nothing you can do with them. A mandoline is the only way to slice the artichoke thin enough to get the right crispy/chewy texture.

chopped romaine and radicchio salad

This is an Italian take on the Middle Eastern salad known as fattoush. It's filled with colors and textures, and crushed pita chips give it more body than you would expect from a plate of greens. Top it with grilled shrimp or grilled chicken—especially if you brush them with a little spicy Calabrian chile paste—and it's also a super all-in-one lunch dish.

YIELD:
SERVES 4 TO 6

SERVE WITH:
MORTADELLA PIADINI

MAKE THE DRESSING: In a jar with a tight-fitting lid, combine the mustard, Parmigiano-Reggiano, vinegar, olive oil, and salt. Screw on the top and shake vigorously to emulsify. Set aside to let the flavors marry.

PREPARE THE SALAD: In a large bowl, toss together the romaine, radicchio, basil, cucumber, avocado, and pita chips. Pour the dressing over the salad, sprinkle with the salt, and toss gently to coat and combine.

FOR THE DRESSING

2 tablespoons whole-grain mustard

¼ cup freshly grated Parmigiano-Reggiano

1 tablespoon champagne vinegar

3 tablespoons extra-virgin olive oil

¼ teaspoon kosher salt

FOR THE SALAD

2 hearts of romaine lettuce

1 large head radicchio

¼ cup chopped fresh basil

½ English cucumber, peeled and diced

1 avocado, pitted, scooped, and diced

2 cups pita chips, crushed

¼ teaspoon kosher salt

italian carrot salad

Carrot salad is a picnic staple, but when it's made with mayo and raisins, it's often just too cloying. I've swapped out the raisins for tart cranberries and added creaminess with a bit of goat cheese, so it's a lot more refreshing and sophisticated. If you've ever wondered what to do with that souvenir bottle of limoncello in the back of the cupboard, you'll love the way it adds some kick to this carrot salad, too!

YIELD:
SERVES 4

SERVE WITH:
MARINATED SALUMI SANDWICH

In a small saucepan, gently warm the limoncello over medium heat until steam begins to come off the top. It should be hot to the touch but not simmering. Remove from the heat, add the dried cranberries, and cover with plastic wrap. Allow the cranberries to soak for at least 30 minutes or up to an hour. Drain and set aside.

Using the large holes on a box grater, grate the carrots into a medium bowl. Season the carrots with the salt and toss well. Add the soaked cranberries, parsley, lemon juice, and olive oil, and toss again to combine. Crumble the goat cheese over the top and serve.

⅓ **cup limoncello**

½ **cup dried cranberries**

1½ **pounds large carrots, peeled**

1 **teaspoon kosher salt**

½ **cup loosely packed fresh parsley leaves, coarsely chopped**

2 **tablespoons fresh lemon juice**

3 **tablespoons extra-virgin olive oil**

2 **ounces soft goat cheese**

tomato, avocado, and escarole salad

YIELD:
SERVES 4 TO 6

SERVE WITH:
SIMPLE STRACCIATELLA *OR* **LEMON SOLE OREGANATA**

This light salad is the perfect thing to serve with a heavy piece of meat or fried food. It works very well with a veal Milanese or anything that needs a sharp counterpoint to offset a rich or fatty flavor.

1 (8-ounce) container cherry tomatoes, halved

½ cup pitted Castelvetrano olives, quartered

¼ cup fresh mint, chopped

½ teaspoon kosher salt

1 large head escarole, thoroughly washed and dried, dark green leaves removed, remaining leaves chopped into bite-size pieces

1 tablespoon white balsamic vinegar

3 tablespoons extra-virgin olive oil

1 avocado, chilled and diced (see Cook's Notes)

½ cup toasted pine nuts (see Cook's Notes)

In a large bowl, combine the tomatoes, olives, mint, and salt. Add the escarole, vinegar, and olive oil, and toss gently to coat. Just before serving, sprinkle with the avocado and the pine nuts, toss once more, and serve.

COOK'S NOTES: Chilling the avocado before cutting makes it easier to dice and, especially if it is ripe, will keep it from becoming mushy.

Toast the pine nuts in a dry skillet over medium heat, shaking the pan frequently, just until they are starting to become golden, about 3 minutes. Transfer immediately to a plate to cool.

wilted baby kale

YIELD:
SERVES 4 TO 6

SERVE WITH:
ITALIAN CHICKEN AND RICE OR FLOUNDER PICCATA

You'll find this easy, tasty side works with most entrées. The secret to these flavorful greens is the anchovy paste, which amplifies their rustic appeal. To switch it up, you can add dried fruit such as cranberries or chopped apricots. It sounds a bit strange, but the sweet/salty combo is really good. Toasted bread crumbs are another good addition.

3 tablespoons olive oil

2 garlic cloves, chopped

1 teaspoon anchovy paste

¼ teaspoon crushed red pepper flakes

1 large head escarole, thoroughly washed, dried, and chopped into 1-inch pieces

½ teaspoon kosher salt

1 teaspoon grated lemon zest (from ½ lemon)

5 ounces baby kale (see Cook's Note)

¼ cup toasted pine nuts (see Cook's Note, page 222)

Heat a large skillet over high heat. Add the olive oil, garlic, anchovy paste, and red pepper flakes, and cook, stirring often with a wooden spoon, until fragrant and toasted, about 1 minute. Add the escarole and ¼ teaspoon of the salt, and cook, stirring often, until completely wilted and coated in all the flavors of the oil, about 2 minutes. Turn off the heat and add the lemon zest, baby kale, and remaining ¼ teaspoon salt. Toss well to coat and slightly wilt the baby kale. Sprinkle the greens with the pine nuts, toss, and serve.

COOK'S NOTE: Italians would use Tuscan kale, but I prefer baby kale, which is more tender and cooks faster. You could also substitute spinach, if you prefer.

warm mushroom salad fiorentina

Not all salads are light and springlike: this is a warm winter salad that's hearty and slightly sweet. Serve it during the cooler months alongside a fish like roasted salmon or grilled steak. Italians would simplify specify *funghi* here, using whatever meaty mushrooms are in season at their market.

YIELD:
SERVES 4

SERVE WITH:
SPICY LINGUINE WITH WALNUTS AND MINT

Heat a medium straight-sided skillet over medium-high heat. Add the olive oil and continue to heat for another minute. Add the mushrooms to the pan and season with ½ teaspoon of the salt. Cook, stirring every so often, for about 5 minutes, or until the mushrooms are an even golden brown on all sides.

Stir in the cranberries and walnuts. Cook for an additional minute. Turn off the heat and add the arugula and remaining ¼ teaspoon salt to the pan. Toss the arugula gently with the mushroom mixture just until wilted, a minute or less. Serve immediately.

3 tablespoons olive oil

¾ pound meaty mushrooms, such as royal trumpets, cleaned and cut into 1-inch pieces

¾ teaspoon kosher salt

½ cup dried cranberries

⅓ cup chopped toasted walnuts (see Cook's Note, page 75)

4 cups packed baby arugula

zucchini sottolio

YIELD:
MAKES ABOUT 5 CUPS

SERVE WITH:
**CREAMY SWEET CORN WITH
PANCETTA
WHOLE ROASTED FISH**

This is one of my favorite ways to eat veggies. In Italy, preserving vegetables in oil is a classic way to boost their flavor and get a few extra weeks out of the growing season. When you have a jar or two on hand, you'll never be at a loss for a quick side. In many restaurants around Florence, you will see a dish like this one set out on the table with bread, and it can certainly do double duty as a starter or part of an antipasto spread. This recipe works with eggplant, too (I like to grill the eggplant first), and assorted peppers.

1¼ pounds zucchini (about 3 small zucchini), sliced into ⅓-inch rounds

1¼ teaspoons kosher salt

1½ cups plus 1 tablespoon apple cider vinegar

10 fresh mint leaves

10 fresh basil leaves

2 garlic cloves, smashed and peeled

½ teaspoon crushed red pepper flakes

2 to 3 cups extra-virgin olive oil

Place the sliced zucchini in a colander that is set over a bowl. Sprinkle with the salt and toss well to combine. Allow the zucchini to sit for 10 minutes.

Meanwhile, in a medium saucepan, combine 1½ cups of water with 1½ cups of the vinegar and bring to a boil over high heat. Add the salted zucchini to the pot and return the mixture to a boil. Reduce the heat to maintain a simmer and cook for 4 to 5 minutes, or until the zucchini is cooked through but still has a little texture. Drain the zucchini and place it in a large bowl.

Add the remaining 1 tablespoon vinegar, the mint, basil, garlic, and red pepper flakes to the zucchini, and toss well. Add enough olive oil to cover the zucchini and allow the mixture to cool to room temperature. Pack the zucchini in jars or a storage container with a tight-fitting lid, making sure the zucchini is fully covered with the oil. Store in the refrigerator for up to 3 weeks. Serve at room temperature.

grilled treviso with citrus bagna cauda

I love a warm grilled salad; a light char softens the leaves and gives it a smoky flavor. Treviso has a bitter edge, so the sweet citrusy dressing is the perfect pairing. If you can't find Treviso, you can substitute romaine or Belgian endive, but I think the long, purple heads are so elegant.

YIELD:
SERVES 4 TO 6

SERVE WITH:
LEMON WHITE PIZZA
BURRATA WITH NECTARINES
AND CORN

MAKE THE BAGNA CAUDA: Heat the oil in a small sauté pan over medium heat. Add the garlic and anchovies. Cook, stirring often and breaking up the anchovies with a wooden spoon, until they dissolve and the garlic is fragrant and beginning to brown, about 3 minutes. Set aside to cool. Meanwhile, combine the lemon zest, orange zest, lemon juice, orange juice, honey, salt, and pepper in a small bowl. Once the oil mixture is cooled to room temperature, whisk the seasoned oil into the citrus. Allow to mingle for about 10 minutes, then discard the garlic.

Preheat a grill pan over medium-high heat.

Grill the Treviso halves for 3 minutes per side over medium-high heat, until charred and slightly wilted in some spots. Remove the Treviso from the grill and cut out the core. Chop the leaves into bite-size pieces and place them in a medium bowl. Season with the salt. Toss the Treviso with the dressing, sprinkle with the walnuts, and serve.

FOR THE BAGNA CAUDA

3 tablespoons extra-virgin olive oil

3 garlic cloves, smashed and peeled

2 anchovy fillets

1 teaspoon grated lemon zest

1 teaspoon grated orange zest

1 tablespoon fresh lemon juice

1 tablespoon fresh orange juice

1½ teaspoons honey

¼ teaspoon kosher salt

⅛ teaspoon freshly ground black pepper

3 large heads Treviso, halved lengthwise

½ teaspoon kosher salt

½ cup walnuts, coarsely chopped

roasted squash agrodolce

This dish will look so pretty on your table, and the *agrodolce* notes appeal to those who like sweet dishes and to those who like savory, making this a universal crowd-pleaser.

YIELD:
SERVES 6

SERVE WITH:
VEAL SALTIMBOCA
MILANESE-STYLE

Preheat the oven to 450°F.

Using a large knife, cut off a small amount of the top and bottom of the squash. Set the squash on a flat side and cut it in half. Using a large spoon, scoop out the seeds and discard. Cut each half into 5 wedges. Place the squash in a large bowl and add the olive oil, 1 teaspoon of the salt, the cayenne, and cinnamon. Using your hands, toss well to coat. Place the seasoned squash on a rimmed baking sheet and bake for 35 minutes, flipping the squash halfway through, or until golden brown and fork-tender.

In a small saucepan, heat 1 inch of vegetable oil over medium-high heat. Test if the oil is hot enough by touching the tip of a sage leaf to the oil; if it bubbles, the oil is ready for frying. Fry 3 or 4 leaves at a time until the bubbles subside and the leaves become crisp, about 1 minute. Drain in a single layer on a paper towel–lined plate and sprinkle with a pinch of salt.

Melt the butter in a small skillet over medium heat and cook it until the foam subsides and the solids begin to smell nutty and turn brown, 3 to 4 minutes. Cool the butter for 2 minutes.

In a small bowl, whisk together the vinegar and sugar until the sugar dissolves. Whisk in the brown butter using a rubber spatula to get all the brown bits out of the pan. Season with the remaining ½ teaspoon salt. Arrange the squash on a rimmed platter and spoon the vinaigrette over the squash. Dollop with the mascarpone and sprinkle with the almonds and fried sage.

- 2 large acorn squash
- ¼ cup extra-virgin olive oil
- 1½ teaspoons kosher salt, plus more as needed
- ¼ teaspoon cayenne pepper
- ⅛ teaspoon ground cinnamon
- Vegetable oil, for frying
- 15 fresh sage leaves
- ¼ cup (½ stick) unsalted butter, at room temperature
- ¼ cup apple cider vinegar
- 2 tablespoons sugar
- ¼ cup mascarpone cheese
- ¼ cup smoked almonds, coarsely chopped

charred broccoli rabe

YIELD:
SERVES 4

SERVE WITH:
**GRILLED CHICKEN INVOLTINI
CREAMY SWEET CORN
WITH PANCETTA**

Italians generally serve this vegetable just boiled or sautéed with a little garlic, so this is a nice change, and because you cook it all on the grill, there's less cleanup! Grilling makes the edges of the broccoli rabe crispy and gives them a great smoky flavor that goes well with meat or fish.

1 bunch broccoli rabe (about 1 pound), trimmed and washed

2 tablespoons olive oil

¾ teaspoon kosher salt

¼ teaspoon crushed red pepper flakes

Preheat a grill or grill pan over medium-high heat.

Place the broccoli rabe on a sheet of aluminum foil large enough to close and seal over it. Drizzle with the olive oil and sprinkle with the salt and red pepper flakes. Use your hands to toss gently to coat. Bring the sides of the foil up and over the broccoli rabe and crimp the top and sides to seal. Place the packet on the grill directly over the heat source and cook for 8 minutes.

Open the packet, being mindful that the hot steam will escape. Using tongs, transfer the broccoli rabe directly onto the grill grates. Cook for 2 minutes on each side until lightly charred in spots. Remove to a platter and serve.

creamy sweet corn with pancetta

Visitors to my restaurant in Las Vegas order this more than any other side dish, and when we take it off the menu, diners truly get upset . . . people travel especially for it! It's a decadent side and a perfect partner to meat or chicken. When it's in season, the sweet flavor of fresh white corn is especially nice here.

YIELD:
SERVES 4 TO 6

SERVE WITH:
WILTED BABY KALE
SPICY TURKEY POLPETONE

Heat the oil in a large skillet over medium-high heat. Add the pancetta and cook, stirring often with a wooden spoon, until the pancetta is crispy and golden brown, about 5 minutes. Add the shallot, fennel, and red pepper flakes, and cook an additional 3 minutes, or until the vegetables are softened.

Stir in the corn and salt, and mix well to combine and warm through. Add 3 tablespoons of water, then fold in the mascarpone and Parmigiano-Reggiano. Heat just to a simmer, then remove from the heat. Stir in the basil and black pepper, and serve.

2 tablespoons olive oil

¼ pound pancetta, diced

1 shallot, chopped

1 medium fennel bulb, stalks discarded, chopped

¼ teaspoon crushed red pepper flakes

1 (16-ounce) bag sweet corn, thawed, or kernels from 8 ears fresh corn

¾ teaspoon kosher salt

½ cup mascarpone cheese

1 cup freshly grated Parmigiano-Reggiano

¼ cup chopped fresh basil

¼ teaspoon freshly ground black pepper

white beans and tuscan kale

YIELD:
SERVES 6 TO 8

SERVE WITH:
**HERB-ROASTED PORK
TENDERLOIN
GRILLED ARTICHOKES WITH
ANCHOVY MAYONNAISE**

Beans are a pantry staple in most Italian homes, a versatile and filling ingredient Italians rely on the way Americans use potatoes—or even pasta. They're simple, easy to dress up or down, and a cost-effective way to round out a meal. This takes a while to cook, but it's almost all hands-off time, and because it makes a large batch, you can serve it for several meals throughout the week.

2 cups dry white beans, such as cannellini

6 cups filtered or bottled water

1 fresh sage sprig

4 garlic cloves, smashed and peeled

½ cup plus 2 tablespoons extra-virgin olive oil

1 small bunch Tuscan kale, chopped

1¾ teaspoons kosher salt

½ teaspoon crushed red pepper flakes

½ cup freshly grated Parmigiano-Reggiano

In a medium Dutch oven, combine the beans, water, sage, garlic, and 2 tablespoons of the olive oil. Bring to a boil over medium-high heat, then reduce the heat to medium-low to maintain a gentle simmer. Partially cover the pot with a lid and simmer for 1 hour and 20 minutes, stirring occasionally. The beans should be just tender all the way through.

Add the kale, salt, and red pepper flakes to the beans, and stir to combine. Cover the pot and simmer 15 minutes longer, or until the kale is wilted and tender. Stir in the remaining ½ cup olive oil and the grated Parmigiano-Reggiano to finish.

roasted parmigiano-reggiano potatoes

You'll often see potatoes roasted this way in the north of Italy, the home of Parmigiano-Reggiano. They go with just about any entree you can think of—year round. I make them at least three times a week! Kids and adults go nuts for the delectable crust that the cheese makes on the outside of the potatoes.

YIELD:
SERVES 4

SERVE WITH:
CHOPPED ROMAINE AND RADICCHIO SALAD PAN-SEARED SALMON WITH ARTICHOKES AND WHITE WINE

Preheat the oven to 425°F.

Spread the potatoes on a rimmed baking sheet. Drizzle with the olive oil and sprinkle with the salt and rosemary. Toss well to coat.

Roast the potatoes for 20 minutes. Remove from the oven and, using a metal spatula, toss the hot potatoes. Sprinkle with the Parmigiano-Reggiano and toss again to coat. Return the pan to the oven and roast an additional 10 minutes, tossing again halfway through. Serve warm.

1 pound Yukon Gold potatoes, unpeeled and quartered

¼ cup olive oil

¾ teaspoon kosher salt

¾ teaspoon chopped fresh rosemary

1 cup freshly grated Parmigiano-Reggiano

cheesy mashed potatoes

There's a lot of cheese in this dish, so much, in fact, that it's really more of a potato puree with just enough potatoes to hold the cheese together. In other words, it's insanely decadent and totally delicious! It's great with a pork loin, a leaner meat, or a filet of beef.

YIELD:
SERVES 8

SERVE WITH:
**WARM MUSHROOM SALAD
FIORENTINA
TRICOLORE STUFFED PORK**

Place the potatoes, rosemary, and garlic in a large saucepan, and cover with cold water. Add a handful of salt and bring to a boil over medium-high heat. Boil until the potatoes are fork-tender, about 15 minutes. Drain well and discard the rosemary sprigs.

Press the potatoes and garlic through a potato ricer back into the saucepan. Add the warmed cream and olive oil. Place the pan back over low heat and stir everything together with a rubber spatula. Add the mozzarella, Parmigiano-Reggiano, and salt to taste, and continue to stir until the mixture is hot, the cheese is melted, and the potatoes are almost stringy in texture. This will take 5 to 10 minutes. Serve hot.

2½ pounds Yukon Gold potatoes, peeled and quartered

3 fresh rosemary sprigs

2 garlic cloves, smashed and peeled

Kosher salt

1½ cups heavy cream, warmed

¼ cup extra-virgin olive oil

1 pound fresh mozzarella cheese, shredded

1 cup freshly grated Parmigiano-Reggiano

creamy polenta with spinach

YIELD:
SERVES 6 TO 8

SERVE WITH:
**ENDIVE, PANCETTA, AND TOMATO SALAD
ITALIAN SPRINGTIME LAMB**

If there is an Italian equivalent to mashed potatoes, something you can serve with—or under—just about anything, it's got to be polenta. Maybe it's the Italian in me, but I like its texture and the sweet corn flavor a lot more. Spinach makes it somewhat virtuous and also so pretty. This is rich, so serve it in small portions.

3 cups low-sodium chicken broth

2 tablespoons olive oil

2 garlic cloves, smashed and peeled

1½ cups quick-cooking polenta

1 teaspoon kosher salt

1½ cups freshly grated Parmigiano-Reggiano

1 cup freshly grated pecorino cheese

8 ounces mascarpone cheese

3 tablespoons unsalted butter

5 ounces baby spinach, roughly chopped

In a Dutch oven, combine the chicken broth, olive oil, and garlic with 2 cups water, and bring to a boil over medium-high heat. Reduce the heat to medium-low and whisk in the polenta. Season with the salt and cook for 5 minutes, stirring occasionally with a wooden spoon. Stir in the Parmigiano-Reggiano, pecorino, mascarpone, and butter. Cook for 3 minutes, stirring often. Fold in the spinach and cook until wilted, about 3 minutes longer. Remove from the heat and serve immediately.

roasted squash with cherries and pistachios

YIELD:
SERVES 4

SERVE WITH:
**MARINATED BISTECCA
FIORENTINA
CHARRED BROCCOLI RABE**

When I think about "eating the rainbow," dishes like this one immediately come to mind. It's a feast of colors, textures, and flavors. The sweet balsamic vinegar and piney rosemary scent remind me of the holidays. This is substantial enough to be a main dish for a vegetarian.

FOR THE VINAIGRETTE

3 tablespoons white balsamic vinegar

3 tablespoons extra-virgin olive oil

½ teaspoon kosher salt

FOR THE SQUASH

2 large acorn squash, halved, seeded, and cut into wedges

2 tablespoons olive oil

1 teaspoon kosher salt

2 fresh rosemary sprigs

2 garlic cloves, unpeeled and smashed

¼ cup dried tart cherries

½ cup roasted pistachios

2 cups baby arugula

2 ounces Gorgonzola dolce, crumbled

Preheat the oven to 400°F.

MAKE THE VINAIGRETTE: In a medium bowl, whisk together the vinegar, olive oil, and salt. Set aside.

PREPARE THE SQUASH: Place the squash wedges on a rimmed baking sheet. Drizzle with the olive oil and salt. Add the rosemary sprigs and garlic. Cover the baking sheet tightly with a sheet of aluminum foil. Roast the squash for 35 to 40 minutes, or until the tip of a knife easily pierces the squash. Remove the sheet from the oven and drizzle three-quarters of the vinaigrette over the squash. Allow it to cool and absorb the dressing for about 10 minutes.

To the bowl with the remaining vinaigrette, add the cherries, pistachios, and arugula. Toss gently to coat. Place the marinated squash wedges on a platter and top with the dressed greens. Sprinkle with crumbled Gorgonzola and serve.

OLIVE OIL AND HONEY
PANNA COTTA

WHITE CHOCOLATE
ORZO PUDDING

CHIANTI AFFOGATO

BLACK-AND-WHITE
BROWNIE ICE CREAM
CAKE

MASCARPONE SORBETTO
WITH ROSEMARY HONEY

SPRITZER SLUSHY

FENNEL UPSIDE-DOWN
CAKE

ANGEL FOOD CAKE WITH
CHOCOLATE-HAZELNUT
FROSTING

POUND CAKE
WITH LIMONCELLO
ZABAGLIONE

PEACH AND ALMOND
CROSTATA

MASCARPONE CANNOLI
CHEESECAKE

SALTED DARK
CHOCOLATE CHUNK
BROWNIES

CHOCOLATE CHERRY
SHORTBREAD COOKIES

HEARTY CHOCOLATE
CHIP COOKIES

sweets

Desserts, and sweets in general, play a smaller role in the daily lives of Italians than they do for Americans. As kids, my brother, sister, and I may have had a piece of chocolate here or there, or a trip to the gelato shop on weekends, but true desserts were reserved for special occasions in my family. On the whole, Italian desserts are often not terribly sweet and were designed to use up leftover fruits, broken cookies, extra nuts, or even excess produce from the garden, like fennel; you'd rarely see an Italian cook just make a pan of brownies for no reason. However, if you're like me and want the last impression you leave on your friends and family—and your palate for that matter—to be a sweet one, you can't live without dessert. In the spirit of authenticity, many of these confections, like the chewy Chocolate Cherry Shortbread Cookies (page 279) or the Olive Oil and Honey Panna Cotta (page 249), have an underlying savory note and aren't over-the-top sweet. But I couldn't resist including a few of my current favorites, sweets you probably wouldn't encounter in Italy. Trust me, you'll thank me anyway. After all, to paraphrase Julia Child, a meal without dessert is just a meeting.

olive oil and honey panna cotta

I haven't included panna cotta recipes in many of my books because, to be honest, panna cotta isn't my favorite dessert. However, I'm clearly in the minority, because you find it on the menu of just about every Italian restaurant, both here and in Italy. This rendition has a slightly spicy bite from the olive oil, which makes it a little bit unusual and less like nursery food. Use a grassy green olive oil and top it with some flake salt and a drizzle of the same oil to play up the distinctive flavor if you like.

YIELD:
SERVES 6

SERVE WITH:
GRILLED TREVISO WITH
CITRUS BAGNA CAUDA
VEAL SALTIMBOCCA
MILANESE-STYLE

Pour the water into a small bowl and sprinkle the gelatin over it. Stir to combine. Set aside to soften for 5 minutes.

Scrape the softened gelatin into a medium saucepan and add the heavy cream, honey, vanilla, lemon zest, and salt. Bring to a simmer over medium heat, stirring with a rubber spatula to dissolve the gelatin and honey. Simmer for 2 minutes. Remove the mixture from the heat.

Stir the olive oil into the cream mixture and, using an immersion blender, blend until combined and emulsified. Stir in the milk. If a large amount of froth has formed on the surface, use a small ladle to skim it off and discard as much of the foam as possible. Divide the mixture among 6 small ramekins or a shallow 1-quart dish. Cover with plastic wrap and refrigerate for at least 5 hours, or until the mixture is set.

Serve topped with fresh raspberries and an extra drizzle of honey, if desired.

¼ cup cold water

1 (0.25-ounce) package powdered gelatin

2 cups heavy cream

⅓ cup raw honey, plus more for drizzling

½ teaspoon pure vanilla extract

½ teaspoon grated lemon zest

¼ teaspoon kosher salt

⅓ cup extra-virgin olive oil

1 cup whole milk

Fresh raspberries, for garnish (optional)

white chocolate orzo pudding

YIELD:
SERVES 6 TO 8

SERVE WITH:
PAPPA AL POMODORO OR FLANK STEAK WITH ROASTED GRAPES AND MUSHROOMS

My grandmother made a lot of rice puddings, but it was never really my favorite dessert because it was a bit bland and the texture was not that appealing. When I added the crunch of crumbled cookies to contrast with the velvety smoothness of white chocolate, though, it was a whole new ball game. Substituting rice-shaped pasta for the rice is a fun twist that makes the pudding even smoother, and it's a good way to use up that partial box of pasta you've got on your shelf.

4 cups whole milk

½ teaspoon kosher salt

3 tablespoons sugar

1 cinnamon stick

½ teaspoon pure vanilla extract

1 cup orzo pasta

1 teaspoon orange zest (from ½ orange)

¾ cup white chocolate chips, such as Guittard

½ cup crushed amaretti cookies

In a medium saucepan or Dutch oven, bring the milk, salt, sugar, cinnamon stick, and vanilla to a simmer over medium heat. Stir in the pasta and reduce the heat to low to maintain a gentle simmer. Cook, stirring often, for 12 to 14 minutes, or until the pasta is cooked and the liquid is beginning to thicken slightly. There will still be a good amount of liquid in the pan.

Stir in the orange zest and white chocolate chips, and continue stirring until the chocolate is melted. Allow the mixture to cool to room temperature, about 20 minutes, stirring occasionally to prevent a skin from forming over the surface. Spoon the pudding into 6 to 8 custard cups or ramekins, cover with plastic wrap, and refrigerate until chilled. Serve with crushed amaretti cookies sprinkled on top.

chianti affogato

In a traditional *affogato*, gelato is "drowned" in espresso, and it's a fun and quick way to have your dessert and coffee at the same time. In this fancied-up version, mulled wine replaces the coffee. The rich blend of warm spices in the wine evokes the holidays and the flavors of cranberry sauce—my favorite part of Thanksgiving! It's luxurious, but not too heavy after a big meal.

YIELD:
SERVES 6

SERVE WITH:
**CRISPY CHICKEN THIGHS WITH PEPPERS AND CAPERS
CREAMY POLENTA WITH SPINACH**

In a medium saucepan, combine the wine, cinnamon stick, peppercorns, turbinado sugar, basil, orange zest, and salt. Place over medium heat and bring to a simmer, stirring occasionally with a wooden spoon to help dissolve the sugar. Reduce the heat to medium-low to maintain a gentle simmer and cook the mixture for 5 minutes. Turn off the heat and allow it to steep for 5 minutes. Strain the liquid through a fine-mesh strainer into a pitcher.

Divide the gelato among 6 coffee cups or small glasses. Pour the warm liquid over each portion and serve with demitasse spoons.

2 cups Chianti wine

1 cinnamon stick

¼ teaspoon black peppercorns

¼ cup turbinado sugar

2 fresh basil sprigs

½ teaspoon grated orange zest (from ½ orange)

⅛ teaspoon kosher salt

1 pint vanilla gelato or ice cream

black-and-white brownie ice cream cake

Semifreddo, a frozen dessert sometimes layered with bits of crumbled cookies or fruit, is considered a special-occasion treat for Italians. It takes quite a bit of time to make one, since the ice cream layers traditionally are made from scratch. With its brownie layers (and store-bought ice cream), my version is a lot quicker to put together, but it still captures the spirit of an authentic Italian semifreddo. For the holidays, Jade loves it when I decorate this with little candy canes. Brownie mix is another shortcut here, and it actually works better than homemade because the brownies don't absorb as much moisture (no one likes a soggy cake!).

YIELD:
SERVES 6 TO 8

SERVE WITH:
**SAUSAGE AND BROCCOLI PIZZA
GRILLED CHICKEN INVOLTINI**

Preheat the oven to 350°F.

Line a rimmed 12 × 8½-inch quarter sheet pan or a 9 × 13-inch baking dish with parchment paper (see Cook's Notes). Spray the paper with nonstick cooking spray and set aside.

In a large bowl, use a rubber spatula to stir together the brownie mix, eggs, liqueur, vegetable oil, and almond extract. Spread the mixture evenly in the prepared pan. Bake for 18 to 20 minutes, or until the brownie is just set. Allow the brownie to cool in the pan for 10 minutes before removing it from the pan to cool completely on a wire rack.

Line a 5 × 9-inch loaf pan with a piece of parchment paper that overhangs each long side by about 2 inches. Remove the pints of ice cream from the freezer for about 10 minutes to soften just slightly (see Cook's Notes).

Cut the cooled brownie sheet into 3 equal 9-inch-long rectangles. Place 1 piece in the bottom of the loaf pan. Scoop the softened

Nonstick cooking spray

1 (18.2-ounce) box dark chocolate fudge brownie mix, such as Duncan Hines

2 large eggs, at room temperature

⅓ cup hazelnut liqueur, such as Frangelico

⅓ cup vegetable oil

½ teaspoon almond extract

1 pint vanilla ice cream

1 pint chocolate–chocolate chip ice cream

1 tablespoon confectioners' sugar (optional)

recipe continues »

COOK'S NOTES: If you bake the brownies in a 9 × 13-inch pan instead of the quarter sheet pan, they will be a little thinner and need a minute or two less in the oven. Trim the rectangles as needed to fit the loaf pan, as they will be slightly larger.

To help soften and spread the ice cream, put half of it in a stand mixer and whip. Add the rest, whip again, and it will spread easily and evenly.

vanilla ice cream onto the brownie and spread it evenly with an offset spatula. Place another brownie rectangle on top of the ice cream and press down gently. Scoop the softened chocolate–chocolate chip ice cream onto that brownie and repeat spreading the ice cream evenly with an offset spatula. Place the last brownie rectangle on top and press firmly. Wrap in plastic wrap. Freeze for at least 5 hours, preferably overnight.

To unmold, run a thin knife along the two short sides of the loaf pan to loosen the cake and turn it out, upside-down, onto a chilled plate. Peel off the parchment and dust with the confectioners' sugar, if desired. Slice the cake and serve.

mascarpone sorbetto with rosemary honey

YIELD:
SERVES 4 TO 6

SERVE WITH:
**WHOLE ROASTED FISH
BITTER RICE**

In the Mediterranean, bowls of thick yogurt or soft cheese like ricotta drizzled with herb-scented or floral honey are served for breakfast, snacks, and dessert. I stole the idea for this creamy *sorbetto* from that yummy flavor combination. It's the perfect afternoon treat and a great way to end a seafood meal. In the summer months, I might even have it for breakfast.

¾ cup sugar

1 teaspoon grated lemon zest

2 tablespoons fresh lemon juice

⅛ teaspoon kosher salt

1½ cups mascarpone cheese, at room temperature

¾ cup orange blossom honey

3 fresh rosemary sprigs

In a small saucepan combine the sugar with 1¼ cups water. Place over medium-low heat and bring to a simmer, stirring occasionally with a rubber spatula to help dissolve the sugar. Simmer for 1 minute. Remove from the heat and add the lemon zest, lemon juice, and salt. Cool slightly.

In a medium bowl, whisk the mascarpone to loosen it. Add the slightly cooled lemon syrup and whisk until smooth. Cool completely to room temperature, about 30 minutes.

Prepare your ice cream maker. Whisk the mascarpone mixture once more to incorporate the ingredients and freeze according to the manufacturer's directions. Transfer the sorbetto to a storage container and place in the freezer to freeze completely.

Meanwhile, combine the honey and rosemary in a small skillet and stir in 2 tablespoons water. Bring to a simmer over low heat and simmer gently for about 5 minutes. Strain the honey through a fine-mesh strainer, discarding the herb sprigs, and cool to room temperature.

To serve, scoop the sorbetto into a champagne coupe and drizzle with some of the rosemary honey.

spritzer slushy

In the south of Italy from Capri to Amalfi, the Aperol Spritz is the drink of summer, a lightly alcoholic cocktail made with bitter orange liqueur and sparkling wine. It's even more refreshing as a slushy. If you don't want to bother with scraping the frozen mixture to get that granular texture, you could simply pour the mixture into small paper cups and add wooden sticks when it begins to harden. Either way it makes a great treat for the grown-ups at a pool party. The Prosecco turns it into a dessert cocktail, but if you want, you can just serve it in a small bowl with a demitasse spoon.

YIELD:
SERVES 8

SERVE WITH:
LEMON WHITE PIZZA
GRILLED SCALLOPS WITH
PROSCIUTTO AND BASIL

In a small saucepan, combine the orange juice, lemon juice, sugar, and salt. Warm over medium heat to just below a simmer, stirring with a wooden spoon to help dissolve the sugar. Once the sugar is dissolved, remove the pan from the heat and stir in the liqueur. Set aside to cool completely.

Pour the mixture into an 8-inch baking dish and freeze for 4 hours, or until completely solid. Using a fork, scrape the surface of the frozen mixture to form large shards of ice. Spoon about ½ cup of the mixture into a champagne coupe and top with prosecco.

2 cups freshly squeezed orange juice (from about 8 oranges)

3 tablespoons freshly squeezed lemon juice (from 2 lemons)

⅓ cup sugar

¼ teaspoon kosher salt

2 cups bitter orange liqueur, such as Aperol

1 (750 ml) bottle of prosecco

fennel upside-down cake

Fennel turns up in lots of recipes in Italy because its licorice-y flavor can go either sweet or savory. Its underlying sweetness really develops when you poach it in a sugar syrup, so I thought it would be fun to borrow the American tradition of upside-down cake and combine it with this unexpected ingredient. The base is a simple, elegant cake that my family used to serve with coffee in the afternoon or for Sunday brunch. The finishing touch of raspberry sauce is a must, because it adds some tang and the color combo is fantastic.

YIELD:
SERVES 8

SERVE WITH:
**SHAVED FENNEL AND ARTICHOKE SALAD
PENNE WITH PORK RAGU**

---

1 teaspoon olive oil

FOR THE FENNEL

½ cup sugar

2 small or 1 large fennel bulb, halved lengthwise and cut into ⅛-inch-thick half-moons, fronds reserved for garnish

¼ teaspoon ground fennel seed (see Cook's Note, page 207)

⅛ teaspoon kosher salt

1 tablespoon fresh lemon juice (from 1 lemon; see Cook's Note)

FOR THE CAKE

1 cup all-purpose flour

½ cup sugar

¼ teaspoon baking powder

¼ teaspoon baking soda

¼ teaspoon salt

½ cup whole milk, at room temperature

2 large eggs, at room temperature

⅔ cup extra-virgin olive oil

1 teaspoon grated lemon zest

¼ teaspoon fennel pollen or ground fennel seed

FOR THE SAUCE

⅓ cup seedless raspberry jam

1 tablespoon fresh lemon juice

2 tablespoons warm water

Preheat the oven to 350°F. Grease an 8-inch cake pan with 1 teaspoon olive oil.

PREPARE THE FENNEL: In a medium saucepan, dissolve the sugar in ¾ cup water over medium heat, stirring occasionally, with a wooden spoon. Add the fennel, fennel seed, salt, and lemon juice, and bring to a simmer. Reduce the heat to medium-low and cook for 15 minutes, or until the liquid is reduced by three-quarters.

recipe continues »

Spread the candied fennel and syrup evenly over the bottom of the prepared pan. Set aside to cool slightly.

WHILE THE FENNEL POACHES, MAKE THE CAKE BATTER: Whisk together the flour, sugar, baking powder, baking soda, and salt in a medium bowl. In a separate bowl, whisk together the milk, eggs, olive oil, lemon zest, and fennel pollen. Add the dry ingredients to the wet and whisk until just combined. Pour the batter evenly over the slightly cooled candied fennel. Bake for 30 minutes, or until a toothpick inserted in the middle of the cake comes out clean. Cool for 10 minutes in the pan. Invert the cake onto a plate to cool completely.

MAKE THE SAUCE: In a small bowl whisk together the jam, lemon juice, and warm water.

Sprinkle the cake with a few sprigs of the reserved fennel fronds, slice the cake into wedges, and serve with a spoonful of the sauce.

angel food cake with chocolate-hazelnut frosting

YIELD:
SERVES 10

SERVE WITH:
**LEMON AND PEA ALFREDO
SLOW-ROASTED SALMON**

If you're looking for a dessert that blows people away, but you don't consider yourself much of a baker, you've come to the right place. This recipe transforms a store-bought cake into a showstopper, and all without turning on the oven or heating up your house. It's also a great quick birthday cake, especially if you decorate it with fresh flowers.

½ cup bittersweet chocolate chips

½ cup chocolate-hazelnut spread, such as Nutella

1 teaspoon instant espresso powder

⅛ teaspoon kosher salt

1½ cups heavy cream

1 (9-inch) store-bought angel food cake or pound cake, cut in 2 equal layers

Edible flowers, preferably organic, for garnish (optional)

Place the chocolate chips, chocolate-hazelnut spread, instant espresso, and salt in a medium bowl and stir to combine. Pour the heavy cream into a small saucepan and place over medium-high heat. Heat until small bubbles start to form around the edge of the pan. Pour the hot cream over the chocolate mixture and let stand for 1 minute. Beginning in the center of the bowl, whisk it in small circles, stirring the mixture until it is combined and smooth. Cool to room temperature. Cover with plastic wrap and refrigerate for 2 to 3 hours.

To make the frosting, use a hand mixer on medium speed to beat the chilled chocolate mixture for 5 minutes, or until it is light, slightly thickened, and spreadable.

To assemble the cake, place the bottom cake layer on a serving plate or cake stand. Spread one-quarter of the frosting on top of the cake and smooth to within ¼ inch of the edge and center hole. Place the second cake layer on top of the frosting, smooth-side up, and gently press to spread the frosting to the edges. Use a rubber spatula to spoon the rest of the frosting on top of the cake. Using a small offset spatula and starting in the middle of the cake, push the extra frosting across the top and over the sides of the cake. Smooth the sides with the offset spatula to cover them completely. Smooth the top of the cake or make a decorative pattern. Refrigerate until ready to serve.

Remove the cake from the refrigerator 15 minutes before serving. Decorate with colorful edible flowers, if desired.

pound cake with limoncello zabaglione

Limoncello (lemon liqueur) is a specialty of Positano and the Amalfi coast, a digestif that is usually served as an after-dinner drink to help settle the stomach. I like to use it to make desserts that keep your tummy happy, too! Here, I've added a double dose, macerating berries in a touch of limoncello, and using it to flavor a cooked custard sauce, or zabaglione, to dress up a store-bought pound cake for a fast and fun dinner party dessert.

YIELD:
SERVES 4

SERVE WITH:
FARRO AND WHITE BEAN MINESTRONE
LAMB OSSO BUCO

PREPARE THE BERRIES: In a medium bowl, mix together the berries, limoncello, sugar, and lemon juice. Crush the berries gently with the back of a fork. Cover and set aside for at least 30 minutes to let the juices develop and the flavors mingle.

MAKE THE SAUCE: Bring a medium saucepan with 2 inches of water to a simmer over medium heat. In a medium heatproof bowl that fits comfortably over the saucepan without touching the water, use a hand mixer to beat together the egg yolks, limoncello, lemon zest, lemon juice, and sugar on low speed until smooth and incorporated. Place the bowl over the simmering water and continue to beat constantly on low speed over the heat for about 10 minutes, or until a thick ribbon falls onto the mixture when the beaters are lifted from the bowl. Remove the bowl from the heat and continue to beat for another 2 minutes to cool the mixture slightly and prevent the yolks from cooking. Cool to room temperature.

TO SERVE, place a slice of pound cake on each serving plate. Top with a spoonful of berries and a dollop of the limoncello zabaglione.

FOR THE BERRIES

2 cups mixed berries

2 teaspoons limoncello

2 teaspoons sugar

1 tablespoon fresh lemon juice

FOR THE SAUCE

4 large egg yolks

3 tablespoons limoncello

½ teaspoon grated lemon zest

½ teaspoon fresh lemon juice

3 tablespoons sugar

½ (10.75-ounce) pound cake, homemade or store-bought, cut in ¾-inch slices

peach and almond crostata

YIELD:
SERVES 6 TO 8

SERVE WITH:
**ROMAN SEAFOOD CHOWDER
ENDIVE, PANCETTA, AND
TOMATO SALAD**

You get the best of both a crisp and a pie in this rustic crostata. My favorite part is the streusel, a real treat for almond lovers like me, thanks to a bit of almond paste as well as slivered almonds. It's especially nice after a big lunch. I've used frozen peaches for convenience here, but when peaches are in season, do as the Italians would and use fresh for a truly phenomenal dessert.

FOR THE STREUSEL

½ **cup almond paste, cut in small pieces**

2 **tablespoons (¼ stick) unsalted butter, chilled and cubed**

¼ **cup all-purpose flour**

¼ **teaspoon kosher salt**

¼ **cup slivered almonds**

FOR THE CROSTATA

2 **(10-ounce) bags of frozen sliced peaches, thawed and drained, or 1 pound fresh peaches (about 3 large), peeled and sliced (see Cook's Note)**

2 **tablespoons all-purpose flour**

¼ **cup packed light brown sugar**

¼ **teaspoon almond extract**

¼ **teaspoon ground cinnamon**

1 **(9-inch) round of store-bought pie dough**

1 **large egg, beaten**

Preheat the oven to 400°F. Line a rimmed baking sheet with parchment paper and set aside.

MAKE THE STREUSEL: In a small bowl, combine the almond paste, butter, flour, salt, and almonds. Using your fingers, mix everything together until crumbly. Set aside.

MAKE THE CROSTATA: In a medium bowl, combine the peaches, flour, brown sugar, almond extract, and cinnamon. Mix well with a spoon to combine. Unroll the pie dough onto the prepared baking sheet. Spoon the peach mixture into the center of the dough, leaving a 2-inch border. Fold the border up and over the filling, pleating the dough every inch or so along the way.

Spoon the streusel over the top of the filling and press it down gently; the majority of the peaches will be covered with streusel. Brush the edges of the pie dough with the beaten egg. Bake for 30 to 35 minutes, or until the crust is golden brown and the filling is bubbly. Allow to cool for 15 minutes before slicing.

COOK'S NOTE: If using fresh peaches, dunk them into boiling water for just a few seconds to loosen the skins and make peeling easier.

mascarpone cannoli cheesecake

YIELD:
SERVES 12

SERVE WITH:
**WHOLE ROASTED FISH
WILTED BABY KALE**

In the south of Italy, you will find families who have been making cannoli for generations, and, truly, their pastries are an art form—something even Italians wouldn't necessarily undertake at home. I've incorporated those same great flavors into an elegant cheesecake that's a lot less tricky to make. Italians often use ricotta in their filling. I prefer the silky, smooth texture and tang of cream cheese and a bit of mascarpone, which makes the cheesecake lighter and fluffier.

8 large dry almond anise biscotti or your favorite flavor

¼ cup (½ stick) unsalted butter, melted

½ teaspoon kosher salt

2 (8-ounce) packages cream cheese, at room temperature

1 (8-ounce) container mascarpone cheese, at room temperature

¾ cup sugar

1 teaspoon pure vanilla extract

1 teaspoon grated lemon zest

3 large eggs, at room temperature

¾ cup mini semisweet chocolate chips

Italian cherries in syrup, such as Luxardo (optional)

Preheat the oven to 350°F.

In a food processor, pulse the biscotti to fine crumbs. Drizzle in the butter and add ¼ teaspoon of the salt. Pulse until the mixture is the texture of wet sand. Press the mixture into the bottom of a 9-inch springform pan. Bake for 8 minutes, or until the crust is beginning to brown and smells toasted. Set aside to cool while you make the filling. Reduce the oven temperature to 325°F.

In the bowl of a stand mixer fitted with the paddle attachment, beat together the cream cheese, mascarpone, and sugar, scraping down the sides of the bowl occasionally with a rubber spatula, until light and fluffy, about 3 minutes. Add the remaining ¼ teaspoon salt, the vanilla, and lemon zest, and beat again on medium speed until combined. Add the eggs, one at a time, beating until just combined after each addition. Scrape down the sides and mix again. Fold in the chocolate chips by hand.

Spread the cheese mixture evenly over the crust. Bake for 45 to 50 minutes, or until the center of the cake still moves just slightly. Cool on a wire rack for 1 hour before covering with plastic wrap and chilling for at least 4 hours.

To serve, run a knife around the edge of the cheesecake, then release the collar. Serve in thin wedges with a spoonful of cherries.

salted dark chocolate chunk brownies

YIELD:
SERVES 8 TO 10

SERVE WITH:
**SICILIAN TUNA SALAD
SANDWICH
SARDINIAN PASTA SALAD**

As brownies go, this one isn't overly sweet, and it has a dense texture similar to a flourless chocolate cake. The sprinkling of flake salt and coarse sugar on top of the rich brownie gives it a lovely crunch. They are intense, so you can serve these in small portions—or not! It goes really well with the bit of bold red wine left in your glass after a big Sunday dinner.

Nonstick cooking spray

½ cup all-purpose flour

⅓ cup unsweetened cocoa powder

¼ teaspoon kosher salt

½ cup (1 stick) unsalted butter

¾ cup granulated sugar

2 teaspoons pure vanilla extract

2 large eggs, at room temperature

½ cup bittersweet chocolate chunks

1 teaspoon flake salt, such as Maldon

2 teaspoons turbinado or raw sugar

Preheat the oven to 350°F. Spray an 8-inch baking dish with nonstick cooking spray.

In a small bowl, whisk together the flour, cocoa powder, and kosher salt. Set aside.

Place the butter in a medium bowl and microwave it in 20-second increments until just melted, about 40 seconds. Whisk in the granulated sugar and vanilla. Whisk in the eggs, one at a time, mixing until smooth after each addition. Using a rubber spatula, fold in the flour mixture until just a few streaks of dry ingredients remain. Add the chocolate chunks and fold a few more times to incorporate.

Pour the batter into the prepared pan and sprinkle with the flake salt and turbinado sugar. Bake for 28 minutes, or until a toothpick inserted in the center comes out with just a few moist crumbs. Allow to cool completely in the pan before cutting into squares.

chocolate cherry shortbread cookies

When I was a kid, my mom always let me dip my cookies in her glass of *moscato,* a sweet effervescent wine most often served with dessert, and to this day I still love that combination of flavors. These cookies are quite sophisticated and multidimensional, with chocolate chips and cherries as well as a hint of pink peppercorns.

YIELD:
MAKES 1½ DOZEN COOKIES

SERVE WITH:
CHIANTI AFFOGATO *OR* **DESSERT WINE**

In a medium bowl, whisk together the flour, cocoa powder, peppercorns, and salt. Set aside.

Place the butter and ⅓ cup of the sugar in a large bowl. Using a mixer, beat the mixture until pale, light, and fluffy, about 2 minutes. Add the egg yolks and beat an additional minute. Add the flour mixture in two additions, beating on low speed until just combined after each addition. Stir in the cherries and chocolate chips by hand.

Place a piece of plastic wrap on a clean, dry surface. Form the dough into a log about 2 inches wide on the plastic wrap and wrap tightly. Refrigerate for at least an hour or freeze for up to 3 months (see Cook's Note).

Preheat the oven to 350°F.

Using a sharp, thin knife, cut the dough into ⅓-inch slices and place them 1 inch apart on an ungreased baking sheet. Sprinkle the cookies evenly with the remaining 2 tablespoons sugar. Bake for 25 minutes, or until just set. Cool completely on the baking sheet before transferring to an airtight container for storage.

- 1½ cups all-purpose flour
- ⅓ cup unsweetened cocoa powder
- ½ teaspoon pink peppercorns, crushed
- ½ teaspoon kosher salt
- ¾ cup (1½ sticks) unsalted butter, at room temperature
- ⅓ cup plus 2 tablespoons sugar
- 2 large egg yolks, at room temperature
- ¼ cup dried cherries, chopped
- ¼ cup semisweet chocolate chips

COOK'S NOTE: Slice-and-bake cookies like these are great to store in the freezer; just wrap the dough logs extra well in plastic and freeze, then bake as many or as few as you want whenever you need an oven-fresh treat in a hurry.

hearty chocolate chip cookies

YIELD:
MAKES 12 (3½-INCH) COOKIES

SERVE WITH:
GRILLED CHICKEN AND
BROCCOLI PESTO PANINI
POSITANO PIZZAS

I love the chocolate chip cookies at Levain Bakery in New York City. They are dense, gooey, *huge*! I've been trying to re-create them since the first time I tasted them, and I think I've gotten pretty close. My version uses both bittersweet and semisweet chocolate chips to satisfy Jade's palate as well as mine. There's nothing Italian about this one at all, frankly, but I wouldn't deprive you of something so incredibly yummy! They also freeze well; simply put them in the microwave for 5 to 10 seconds to soften them after you take them out of the freezer.

3 cups bread flour

1 teaspoon baking powder

½ teaspoon baking soda

½ teaspoon kosher salt

1 cup (2 sticks) unsalted butter, chilled and cubed

1 cup packed light brown sugar

1 cup granulated sugar

2 large eggs, chilled

2 teaspoons pure vanilla extract

1 cup bittersweet chocolate chips

½ cup semisweet chocolate chips

COOK'S NOTE: It's important for the dough to be completely frozen when you put the cookies in the oven or they will spread too much and not have a soft, chewy interior.

In a large bowl, whisk together the flour, baking powder, baking soda, and salt. Set aside.

In the bowl of a stand mixer fitted with the paddle attachment, beat the cold butter on medium speed about 1 minute to soften slightly. Add the brown sugar and granulated sugar, and mix until incorporated. Add the eggs and the vanilla. Mix on medium-low speed until the mixture looks separated. Turn off the machine and add the dry ingredients. Mix on low speed just until the dough comes together. Turn off the machine and fold in the chips by hand using a rubber spatula.

Drop ½ cup size mounds of the dough onto 2 parchment-lined baking sheets; you should be able to fit 6 cookies on each sheet. Place the baking sheets in the freezer for 1 hour (see Cook's Note).

Preheat the oven to 375°F.

Transfer the baking sheets directly from the freezer to the oven and bake the cookies for 18 to 20 minutes, or until golden brown around the edges and beginning to brown on top but still slightly underbaked in the middle. Let the cookies cool on the baking sheets for 5 minutes and then transfer to a wire rack to cool completely.

acknowledgments

Writing a cookbook that celebrates my homeland is long overdue. I've visited family in Rome with Jade over the years and I've shot several shows in Italy, so it felt like the perfect time to embrace my roots and create a family-inspired Italy cookbook based on the foods I've been eating since I was a kid. My deepest thanks to the following people who helped make this dream possible:

First and foremost, I am indebted to my loving and supportive family. Jade, Mom, and Ivan—I don't know what I would have done without your knowledge of Rome and willingness to explore with me. My aunt Raffy inspired some of the recipes, especially those in the weekend chapter.

Pam Krauss—thanks for your guidance and helping me get La Dolce Vita on paper.

Lish Steiling—my right arm and left arm. I always appreciate your patience, your passion, and your diligence.

Julie Morgan and Sam Saboura—you always keep me looking and feeling like Sophia Loren even after a week full of pasta, gelato, and no sleep. Julie, thank you for countless shakeratos—and to both of you for endless laughter.

Natasha Wynnyk and Lindsey Galey—the two little birds who keep me in line. I so appreciate your young wisdom and lightheartedness.

Aubrie Pick—you were as skilled in the studio as you were tramping through the narrow streets of Rome. Thank you for your amazing eye and ability to capture the small moment. To your lovely team as well—thank you Bessma Khalaf and Cortney Munna.

Alicia Buszczak—thank you for making the props look as good as the food. And to your wonderful assistant Masha Nova.

Sophie Clark—thank you for helping keep Lish sane.

Michael Speagle—thanks for letting me show you my Rome (and for the bag holding!).

Thanks also to my lovely business team: Eric Greenspan, Jon Rosen, and Suzanne Gluck; to my publishing team at Clarkson Potter: Maya Mavjee, David Drake, Aaron Wehner, Doris Cooper, Marysarah Quinn, Kate Tyler, Donna Passannante, Nina Caldas, Stephanie Davis, Jana Branson, and the inimitable Amy Boorstein.

A special thanks to some of our favorite spots in Rome: Eitch Borromini for the gorgeous sunsets; La Buvette, for the endless Aperol spritzes and shakeratos; and Antica Enoteca, for Jade's favorite Bolognese and hand-sliced prosciutto. And lastly, our gratitude to Le Creuset, for the beautiful kitchenwares, and Heath Ceramics, for the gorgeous bowls (I even kept the pink one!).

index

Note: Page references in *italics* indicate photographs.

A

Almond and Peach Crostata, 272, *273*
Anchovy(ies)
  buying, 14
  Citrus Bagna Cauda, 227
  Mayonnaise, *22, 23*
Aperitivi, in Italy, 33
Apricot Mostarda, *38, 39*
Arancini, Crab, *46, 47*–48
Artichoke(s)
  and Fennel, Shaved, Salad, 218
  Grilled, with Anchovy
    Mayonnaise, *22, 23*
  and White Wine, Pan-Seared
    Salmon with, 150, *151*
Arugula
  Calamari Panzanella, 70, *71*
  Candied Lemon Salad, 144–45
  and Pancetta, Cacio e Pepe with,
    108, 109
  Warm Mushroom Salad
    Fiorentina, 225
Asparagus
  with Grilled Melon Salad, 216,
    217
  and Mushroom Farrotto, 178, *179*
Avocado(s)
  Tomato, and Escarole Salad, 222
  Tramezzini (Italian Tea
    Sandwiches), 102–3
  White Bean Dip, 25

B

Bacon. *See also* Pancetta
  Creamy Lobster Linguine, 177
Basil Pesto, 73
Bean(s)
  Fava, and Chianti, Spaghetti
    with, 168, *169*
  Sardinian Pasta Salad, 68–69
  White, and Farro Minestrone, 65
  White, and Tuscan Kale, 236, *237*

White, Avocado Dip, 25
White, Spread, 76, *77*
Beef
  Barolo-Braised Short Ribs, *180*,
    181–82, *183*
  Flank Steak with Roasted
    Grapes and Mushrooms,
    140, 141
  Marinated Bistecca Fiorentina,
    193
  Sartu di Risi, *158*, 159–61
  Spicy Lamb Bolognese, *162*,
    163–64
  Ziti Stufati, *172*, 173–75
Berries. *See also specific berries*
  Pound Cake with Limoncello
    Zabaglione, 270, *271*
Bread
  Calamari Panzanella, 70, *71*
  -Crumb Gremolata, 189–90
  Mortadella Piadina, 101
  Pane Pomodoro, 66, *67*
  Pappa al Pomodoro, *58, 59*
  Salad, Italian Sheet-Pan Chicken
    with, *132*, 133–34
Broccoli Pesto, 74
Broccoli Rabe, Charred, 232, *233*
Brownies, Salted Dark Chocolate
    Chunk, 276, *277*
Bruschetta
  with Burrata and Kale Salsa
    Verde, 97
  Mozzarella and Strawberry, 98,
    99

C

Cakes
  Angel Food, with Chocolate-
    Hazelnut Frosting, 266, *267*
  Black and White Brownie Ice
    Cream, *254*, 255–56
  Fennel Upside-Down, *262*,
    263–64, *265*
  Pound, with Limoncello
    Zabaglione, 270, *271*
Calabrian chile paste, 14

Carrot Salad, Italian, 220, *221*
Cauliflower Soup with Spicy
    Salami, 64
Cheese. *See also* Parmigiano-
    Reggiano
  Antipasti in a Jar, 28, *29*
  Bruschetta with Burrata and Kale
    Salsa Verde, 97
  Burrata with Nectarines and
    Corn, 26, *27*
  Cacio e Pepe with Pancetta and
    Arugula, *108, 109*
  Cheesy Mashed Potatoes, 241
  ciliegine, about, 14–15
  Creamy Polenta with Spinach,
    242, *243*
  Fennel Gratin Pizette, 86
  Goat, and Olives, Potato Crisps
    with, 20, *21*
  Grilled Chicken Involtini, *200*,
    201
  Ham and Ricotta Pinwheels, 49
  Lemon White Pizza, 80
  Marinated Salami Sandwich,
    72, 73
  Mascarpone Cannoli
    Cheesecake, 274
  Mascarpone Sorbetto with
    Rosemary Honey, 258
  Mortadella Piadina, 101
  Mozzarella and Strawberry
    Bruschetta, 98, *99*
  Pecorino, about, 137
  Positano Pizzas, *88, 89*
  Sardinian Pasta Salad, 68–69
  Sartu di Risi, *158*, 159–61
  Sausage and Broccoli Pizza, 84
  Smoked Scamorza, Spinach, and
    Pancetta Pizza, *82, 83*
  Sweet Onion Carbonara, 119
  Tramezzini (Italian Tea
    Sandwiches), 102–3
  Tricolore Stuffed Pork, 196
  Veal Saltimbocca Milanese-
    Style, 198, *199*
  Ziti Stufati, *172*, 173–75

285

Cherry(ies)
  Chocolate Shortbread Cookies,
    278, 279
  and Pistachios, Roasted Squash
    with, 244, *245*
Chicken
  Agrodolce, 135
  Grilled, and Broccoli Pesto
    Panini, 74–75
  Grilled, Involtini, *200*, 201
  Hazelnut, 202
  Italian Sheet-Pan, with Bread
    Salad, *132*, 133–34
  and Rice, Italian, 128
  Thighs, Crispy, with Peppers and
    Capers, 130, *131*
Chocolate
  Black and White Brownie Ice
    Cream Cake, *254*, 255–56
  Cherry Shortbread Cookies,
    278, 279
  Chip Cookies, Hearty, 280
  Dark, Chunk Brownies, Salted,
    276, *277*
  -Hazelnut Frosting, Angel Food
    Cake with, 266, *267*
  White, Orzo Pudding, 250, *251*
Coffee breaks, in Italy, 94
Cookies
  Chocolate Cherry Shortbread,
    278, 279
  Hearty Chocolate Chip, 280
Corn
  Creamy Sweet, with Pancetta,
    234, 235
  and Nectarines, Burrata with,
    26, *27*
  and Spicy Sausage, Penne with,
    120
Crostata
  Peach and Almond, 272, *273*
  Savory, *92*, 93
Crostini with Smoked Trout, 96

E
Eggs
  Simple Stracciatella, *60*, 61
  Smoked Scamorza, Spinach, and
    Pancetta Pizza, *82*, 83
  Sweet Onion Carbonara, 119

Endive, Pancetta, and Tomato
  Salad, *214*, 215
Escarole
  and Spicy Sausage Soup, 52, *53*
  Tomato, and Avocado Salad,
    222
  Wilted Baby Kale, 224

F
Farro
  Florentine Prosciutto Broth, 54
  Mushroom and Asparagus
    Farrotto, 178, *179*
  and White Bean Minestrone, 65
Fennel
  and Artichoke, Shaved, Salad,
    218
  Gratin Pizette, 86
  Upside-Down Cake, *262*,
    263–64, *265*

G
Grapes and Mushrooms, Roasted,
  Flank Steak with, *140*, 141

H
Ham. *See also* Prosciutto
  Grappa-Poached Pears with
    Speck, *34*, 35
  Mortadella Piadina, 101
  and Ricotta Pinwheels, 49
  speck, about, 15
Hazelnut
  Chicken, 202
  -Chocolate Frosting, Angel
    Food Cake with, 266, *267*
Honey
  and Olive Oil Panna Cotta, *248*,
    249
  Rosemary, Mascarpone Sorbetto
    with, 258

I
Ice Cream Cake, Black and White
  Brownie, *254*, 255–56

K
Kale
  Baby, Wilted, 224
  Salsa Verde, 97

Tuscan, and White Beans, 236,
  237

L
Lamb
  Bolognese, Spicy, *162*, 163–64
  Italian Springtime, *188*, 189–90
  Osso Buco, *186*, 187
Lemon
  Candied, Salad, 144–45
  Citrus Bagna Cauda, 227
  and Pea Alfredo, 116, *117*
  White Pizza, 80
Limoncello Zabaglione, Pound
  Cake with, *270*, 271

M
Mayonnaise, Anchovy, *22*, 23
Melon, Grilled, with Asparagus
  Salad, 216, *217*
Mortadella Piadina, 101
Mostarda, Apricot, 38, *39*
Mushroom(s)
  and Asparagus Farrotto, 178, *179*
  and Grapes, Roasted, Flank
    Steak with, *140*, 141
  Monkfish Cacciatore, 154

N
Nectarines and Corn, Burrata with,
  26, *27*

O
Olive Oil and Honey Panna Cotta,
  248, 249
Olives
  Antipasti in a Jar, *28*, 29
  Candied Lemon Salad, 144–45
  Castelvetrano, about, 14
  Crispy Chicken Thighs with
    Peppers and Capers, 130, *131*
  and Goat Cheese, Potato Crisps
    with, 20, *21*
  Hazelnut Chicken, 202
  Pan-Seared Branzino with
    Tomato and Capers, 142, *143*
  Salmon with Puttanesca, 148
Onion(s)
  Carbonara, Sweet, 119
  Savory Crostata, *92*, 93

Oranges
    Citrus Bagna Cauda, 227
    Spritzer Slushy, 260, 261

P
Pancetta
    and Arugula, Cacio e Pepe with,
        108, 109
    Creamy Sweet Corn with, 234,
        235
    Endive, and Tomato Salad, 214,
        215
    Smoked Scamorza, and Spinach
        Pizza, 82, 83
    Sweet Onion Carbonara, 119
Panna Cotta, Olive Oil and Honey,
    248, 249
Pantry items, 13–15
Panzanella, Calamari, 70, 71
Parmigiano-Reggiano
    Broth, Tortellini in, 56, 57
    Cacio e Pepe with Pancetta and
        Arugula, 108, 109
    cheese rinds, flavoring with, 14
    Cheesy Mashed Potatoes, 241
    compared with Pecorino, 137
    Creamy Polenta with Spinach,
        242, 243
    Creamy Sweet Corn with
        Pancetta, 234, 235
    crisps, preparing, 54
    Florentine Prosciutto Broth, 54
    Lemon and Pea Alfredo,
        116, 117
    Pomodoro, Penne with, 167
    Potatoes, Roasted, 238, 239
    and Prosciutto Spiced Prunes, 32
    Sartu di Risi, 158, 159–61
    Simple Stracciatella, 60, 61
Pasta
    Cacio e Pepe with Pancetta and
        Arugula, 108, 109
    Creamy Lobster Linguine, 177
    Fusilli with Fresh Pomodoro, 113
    Lemon and Pea Alfredo,
        116, 117
    Mezzi Rigatoni with Butternut
        Squash and Spicy Sausage,
        124, 125
    Orzo with Clams, 122, 123

Penne with Corn and Spicy
    Sausage, 120
Penne with Parmigiano-
    Reggiano Pomodoro, 167
Penne with Pork Ragu, 170–71
Salad, Sardinian, 68–69
Spaghetti with Chianti and Fava
    Beans, 168, 169
Spicy Lamb Bolognese, 162,
    163–64
Spicy Linguine with Walnuts and
    Mint, 110, 111
Spicy Sausage and Escarole
    Soup, 52, 53
Sweet Onion Carbonara, 119
Tortellini in Parmigiano-
    Reggiano Broth, 56, 57
White Chocolate Orzo Pudding,
    250, 251
Ziti Stufati, 172, 173–75
Pea and Lemon Alfredo, 116, 117
Peach and Almond Crostata, 272,
    273
Pears, Grappa-Poached, with
    Speck, 34, 35
Peppers
    and Capers, Crispy Chicken
        Thighs with, 130, 131
    Monkfish Cacciatore, 154
    Salmon with Puttanesca, 148
    Tricolore Stuffed Pork, 196
    Whole Roasted Fish, 211
Pesto, Basil, 73
Pesto, Broccoli, 74
Pizza
    Fennel Gratin Pizette, 86
    Lemon White, 80
    Positano, 88, 89
    regional favorites, in Rome, 90
    Sausage and Broccoli, 84
    Smoked Scamorza, Spinach, and
        Pancetta, 82, 83
Polenta, Creamy, with Spinach,
    242, 243
Pork. See also Bacon; Ham;
    Sausage(s)
    Ragu, Penne with, 170–71
    Tenderloin, Herb-Roasted,
        138–39
    Tricolore Stuffed, 196

Potato(es)
    Cheesy Mashed, 241
    Crisps with Goat Cheese and
        Olives, 20, 21
    Roasted Parmigiano-Reggiano,
        238, 239
Prosciutto
    and Basil, Grilled Scallops with,
        204, 205
    Broth, Florentine, 54
    Candied, 30, 31
    Grilled Chicken Involtini, 200,
        201
    and Parmigiano-Reggiano
        Spiced Prunes, 32
    Tramezzini (Italian Tea
        Sandwiches), 102–3
    Veal Saltimbocca Milanese-
        Style, 198, 199
Prunes, Parmigiano-Reggiano and
    Prosciutto Spiced, 32
Pudding, White Chocolate Orzo,
    250, 251

R
Radicchio
    Bitter Rice, 126, 127
    and Romaine Chopped Salad,
        219
Rice
    Bitter, 126, 127
    and Chicken, Italian, 128
    Crab Arancini, 46, 47–48
    Sartu di Risi, 158, 159–61
Romaine and Radicchio Chopped
    Salad, 219

S
Salads
    Asparagus with Grilled Melon,
        216, 217
    Bread, Italian Sheet-Pan Chicken
        with, 132, 133–34
    Calamari Panzanella, 70, 71
    Candied Lemon, 144–45
    Carrot, Italian, 220, 221
    Chopped Romaine and
        Radicchio, 219
    Endive, Pancetta, and Tomato,
        214, 215

Salads (*continued*)
    Grilled Treviso with Citrus Bagna
        Cauda, 227
    Pasta, Sardinian, 68–69
    Shaved Artichoke and Fennel,
        218
    Tomato, Avocado, and Escarole,
        222
    Warm Mushroom, Fiorentina,
        225
Salami
    finocchiona, about, 14
    Sandwich, Marinated, 72, 73
    Spicy, Cauliflower Soup with,
        64
Salsa Verde, Kale, 97
Sandwiches
    Grilled Chicken and Broccoli
        Pesto Panini, 74–75
    Italian Tea (Tramezzini), 102–3
    Marinated Salami, 72, 73
    Sicilian Tuna Salad, 76, 77
Sausage(s). *See also* Salami
    and Broccoli Pizza, 84
    Mortadella Piadina, 101
    Sartu di Risi, 158, 159–61
    Spaghetti with Chianti and Fava
        Beans, 168, 169
    Spicy, and Butternut Squash,
        Mezzi Rigatoni with, 124, 125
    Spicy, and Corn, Penne with,
        120
    Spicy, and Escarole Soup, 52, 53
Seafood. *See also* Anchovy(ies)
    Calamari Panzanella, 70, 71
    Chowder, Roman, 63
    Crab Arancini, 46, 47–48
    Creamy Lobster Linguine, 177
    Crostini with Smoked Trout, 96
    Flounder Piccata, 149
    Grilled Scallops with Prosciutto
        and Basil, 204, 205
    Grilled Swordfish with Candied
        Lemon Salad, 144–45
    Italian Barbecued Shrimp, 207
    Lemon Sole Oreganata, 152,
        153
    Monkfish Cacciatore, 154
    Mussels in White Wine, 155
    Orzo with Clams, 122, 123

Pan-Roasted Clams, 42, 43
Pan-Seared Branzino with
    Tomato and Capers, 142,
    143
Pan-Seared Salmon with
    Artichokes and White Wine,
    150, 151
Salmon with Puttanesca, 148
Sicilian Tuna Salad Sandwich,
    76, 77
Slow-Roasted Salmon, 208, 209
Spicy Calabrian Shrimp, 40, 41
Tramezzini (Italian Tea
    Sandwiches), 102–3
tuna, buying, 14
Whole Roasted Fish, 211
Sorbetto, Mascarpone, with
    Rosemary Honey, 258
Soups
    Cauliflower, with Spicy Salami,
        64
    Farro and White Bean
        Minestrone, 65
    Florentine Prosciutto Broth, 54
    Pappa al Pomodoro, 58, 59
    Roman Seafood Chowder, 63
    Simple Stracciatella, 60, 61
    Spicy Sausage and Escarole,
        52, 53
    Tortellini in Parmigiano-
        Reggiano Broth, 56, 57
Spinach
    Creamy Polenta with, 242, 243
    Florentine Prosciutto Broth, 54
    Italian Springtime Lamb, 188,
        189–90
    Smoked Scamorza, and Pancetta
        Pizza, 82, 83
    Tricolore Stuffed Pork, 196
Spritzer Slushy, 260, 261
Squash
    Butternut, and Spicy Sausage,
        Mezzi Rigatoni with, 124,
        125
    Roasted, Agrodolce, 230, 231
    Roasted, with Cherries and
        Pistachios, 244, 245
    Zucchini Sottolio, 226
Strawberry and Mozzarella
    Bruschetta, 98, 99

T
Tomato(es)
    Antipasti in a Jar, 28, 29
    Avocado, and Escarole Salad,
        222
    Calamari Panzanella, 70, 71
    and Capers, Pan-Seared
        Branzino with, 142, 143
    Endive, and Pancetta Salad, 214,
        215
    Fennel Gratin Pizette, 86
    Fusilli with Fresh Pomodoro, 113
    Monkfish Cacciatore, 154
    Pane Pomodoro, 66, 67
    Pappa al Pomodoro, 58, 59
    Penne with Parmigiano-
        Reggiano Pomodoro, 167
    Penne with Pork Ragu, 170–71
    Positano Pizzas, 88, 89
    Sartu di Risi, 158, 159–61
    Spicy Lamb Bolognese, 162,
        163–64
    Tramezzini (Italian Tea
        Sandwiches), 102–3
    Ziti Stufati, 172, 173–75
Treviso, Grilled, with Citrus Bagna
    Cauda, 227
Turkey Polpetone, Spicy, 136

V
Veal Saltimbocca Milanese-Style,
    198, 199

W
Walnuts and Mint, Spicy Linguine
    with, 110, 111
White Chocolate Orzo Pudding,
    250, 251
Wine
    Barolo-Braised Short Ribs, 180,
        181–82, 183
    Chianti Affogato, 252, 253
    Spaghetti with Chianti and Fava
        Beans, 168, 169
    Spritzer Slushy, 260, 261

Z
Zabaglione, Limoncello, Pound
    Cake with, 270, 271
Zucchini Sottolio, 226